Teaching Key Stage 2 Music

A complete, step-by-step scheme of work
by Ann Bryant
Suitable for non-specialists and specialists

To buy Faber Music publications or to find out about the full range of titles available please contact your local retailer or Faber Music sales enquiries:

Faber Music Limited, Burnt Mill, Elizabeth Way, Harlow CM20 2HX England
Tel: +44 (0) 1279 82 89 82   Fax: +44 (0) 1279 82 89 83
sales@fabermusic.com   fabermusic.com

FABER *ff* MUSIC

© 2007 by Faber Music Ltd
First published in 2007 by Faber Music Ltd
3 Queen Square London WC1N 3AU
Music and text setting by Barnes Music Engraving Ltd
Photography by Moose Azim and Keven Erickson
Printed in England by Caligraving Ltd
All rights reserved

CD recorded in various locations
Engineered by Mike Skeet; Produced by Leigh Rumsey
Digital tracks created by David Mitchener
℗ 2007 by Faber Music Ltd   © 2007 by Faber Music Ltd

ISBN10: 0-571-52588-1
EAN13: 978-0-571-52588-1

Contents

Pupils' Sheets (photocopiable)

Appendices

Foreword

This scheme will develop musical expertise in both teacher and student. The lesson plans are clear, original and fun with just the right amount of detail and help for the non-musical teacher. With all the demands from other parts of the curriculum, it is realistic in how many music lessons you might expect to achieve

What makes this scheme different is the chance to be flexible and create your own plans using the Mix and Match ideas – giving teachers just the right amount of freedom to plan lessons exactly how they would like them, whilst at the same time enabling them to feel confident that they are delivering a rounded musical education. No worries about not knowing what to do next, or panic that there's only one week left and you haven't finished the scheme! And importantly, this is a scheme that doesn't compartmentalize age groups, but sees the value in repeating musical games and activities at almost any age.

Furthermore, you can plan specifically for your class, going at a pace that suits them; throw in extra activities to reinforce musical concepts where needed or to fill a gap in the week. This flexibility, together with the excellent audio and visual resources makes this scheme way ahead of any other in its approach. My class loved the *Dustman's Drudge* poem and improvising 'splattertonic' music – if you only have funds for one comprehensive scheme, buy this one!

Lisa Behague
Year 4 Teacher and music specialist
Hartley Primary School, Kent

Acknowledgements

My grateful thanks to Liz Clemence, Wendy Heaton and Nick Quiney for their contribution to the preparation of this book – and most especially to David Mitchener, a teacher whose rapport with children is second to none, and whose help to me has been invaluable. Thanks also to all the delegates at workshops and inset, at the Education Show and other venues who have responded so well and given me such positive feedback, and to those teachers who have troubled to contact me via my website to thank me for the other books in the series.

A big thank you to the choir of Bierton Church of England Combined School who took part in the recording and again to David Mitchener, who trained them and made other wonderful contributions to the CD. Also to the following people who took part in the recording: Berkhampstead School, Cheltenham, Gloucester, Director of Music Helen Mackinnon and Years 5 and 6 choir; soloists: Cerys Mather, Susannah Bagnall, Kate McElroy, Jack Riley, Katie Baxter, Rebecca Mackinnon. Also thanks to the children of Gallions Primary School, Newham and Dulwich Preparatory School, Kent who feature in the photographs. Finally, a great big thank you to Leigh Rumsey, my editor at Faber Music, who has been so lovely to work with.

Ann Bryant

Introduction

This book follows on from the Foundation and Key Stage 1 books to complete this scheme of work for primary schools.

Welcome all teachers who know nothing about music, and all those who are specialists but looking for ideas or are short of time. Read this opening chapter, then you're away! This scheme of work has been written with generalists in mind, though it's true that specialists like to use it too, simply because it is a proper music course, tackling skills and concepts which involve being able to read music.

One of the biggest worries for generalists is feeling that you don't have the facility to assess whether or not your lessons have been a success. I have made this book as user-friendly as possible so that the point of the activity is always clear, the course makes sense to you, and your teaching takes shape. This in turn gives you the confidence to assess. You won't be blindly following instructions, simply hoping that you're 'doing it right'! You won't be making a token gesture towards fulfilling the requirements of the National Curriculum (NC) for music. Instead you will be taking charge of your music teaching.

If you are a generalist, it is inevitable that you will get better at delivering music lessons as you become more experienced and get a feel for what works and what doesn't. Try to look at this fact as a positive. I watched someone teaching a lesson recently, in which the children were sent off in groups with one percussion instrument each and a picture as a stimulus to make music. I was keen to arm them with ideas to help them on their way but the teacher sent them straight off with little preamble. When the groups returned to the music room and presented their pieces to the class, the controlled comment after each piece (a balanced mix of positive comments and suggestions for improvement) dealt with these musical concepts far more constructively than would have been possible by discussing them beforehand out of context, when the children were dying to get on with playing the instruments. It transpired that beforehand, the teacher concerned wasn't sure which musical factors would need to be considered, but on hearing the various musical offerings, he was able to do very effective appraisal work. So this 'learning on the job' was a good thing!

In this progressive course, skills can be learnt, developed, reinforced and integrated so that composition, performance, listening and appraising skills are continually woven into the fabric of the children's music education. You will find yourself and the children becoming more and more musical.

There's so much to cover and you can't cover it all!

Some teachers, whether trained musicians or not, have special areas of expertise and/or of enjoyment. If you have a strong love of jazz music for example and know a lot about it, then of course it can only benefit the children if you put an emphasis on jazz in your music lessons. The same applies to any genre of music or indeed to an instrument that you might have a skill for. Within the context of your particular musical focus, it is also important to be sure to develop children's musical skills and to provide a balanced and broad music curriculum. When writing this book I had to decide (within the constraints of 'teaching the teacher', which takes time) what to cover and what, unfortunately, I couldn't cover. I state this partly to demonstrate that there are limits to what you can cover. The most important goal is for you to feel comfortable in your teaching, and for your enthusiasm to breed enthusiasm in the children. This, in turn will breed progress and success.

Four years worth of material in one book – how does that work?

You will probably need two copies of this book to cater for the four year groups. There are five fully detailed lesson plans for each of the four year groups; you should follow these precisely. Then with the understanding and experience of these five key lessons behind you, you will be equipped to make up your own lesson plans using a mixture of activities from Chapter 6, the Mix and Match section (page 63). Chapter 5 (page 56) also provides guidance to help you to achieve this.

The five set lessons that start off each academic year will appear very long. This is because I have tried to equip non-specialists with all the tools they need to be able to continue devising lessons and delivering them confidently and correctly. Your own lesson plans won't necessarily be as long as these, so don't worry!

No need to read music

You will be taught to read and write notation alongside the children. The CDs included in this book will also help. The songs are written out in case you want to play them, but the CD is a useful tool when learning and rehearsing a new song because each song is sung through first and then repeated with just the accompaniment for you and your class to sing along to. There might not be a single child in the class who turns out to be a professional classical musician, but when children in secondary schools are asked what they most want to get out of their music lessons, their highest priority is to be able to read music. The reading and writing of notation is the language of music – your ticket, if you like, to the world of music. How great to be a nurse able to join your hospital choir, to be the only person at your child's toddler group who can pick out a tune, or to dump your 'air' guitar in favour of the real thing!

Using the Enhanced CD (ECD)

All the written resources you will need are included at the back of this book, and you may photocopy them as required. In addition, we have also included them on the ECD so that they can be printed out as required, transferred to acetate for an OHP or projected directly onto a whiteboard. This is preferable when teaching a song as it avoids paper rustling and bad posture (and subsequently poor singing) from bent-over heads.

What if the children coming up into my class are more musically advanced than I am?

If you have little or no musical background and you find the NC music document difficult to understand, and in particular if the children coming up into your class have been following the KS1 scheme of work, you might well fear that their knowledge of crotchets and quavers is already greater than your own (and anyway, isn't a quaver a well-known brand of crisps?). Don't worry! Whether you are an unconfident non-specialist or a busy specialist, this book aims to set you on the path to good music teaching practice, giving specialists the springboards for their own ideas, as well as giving non-specialists the tools with which to feel that they are in charge of their teaching, following a meaningful, progressive course. The most important thing to remember is that the personality of the music teacher counts for a lot. Your energy, enthusiasm and rapport with the children is needed in music lessons arguably more than in any other lesson.

If you are a Year 4 teacher …

If the children are new to this scheme of work so haven't worked through the set lesson plans for Year 3, it is essential that you do this before embarking on the Year 4 lessons. It might take you less than half a term to get through the five lessons, but it is important that you and the children have a solid foundation of knowledge, understanding and skills before embarking on the more challenging Year 4 work. If the children worked from the scheme in Year 3, but *you* are not a musician and are new to the scheme, you will need to take time to study the set lessons for Year 3 to get a clear understanding of the work covered.

If you are a Year 5 teacher …

If the children are new to this scheme of work so haven't worked through the set lesson plans for Years 3 and 4, it is essential that you do this before embarking on the lessons for Year 5. It might take you less than a term to get through the ten lessons, but it is important that you and the children have a solid foundation of knowledge, understanding and skills before embarking on the more challenging Year 5 work. If the children have worked from the scheme for at least a year, but *you* are not a musician and are new to the scheme, you will need to take time to study the set lessons for Years 3 and 4 to get a clear understanding of the work covered.

If you are a Year 6 teacher …

If the children are new to this scheme of work, so haven't worked through the set lesson plans for Years 3, 4 and 5, it is essential that you do that before embarking on the Year 6 lessons. You might well get through the fifteen lessons much more quickly than in a term and a half, but it is important that you and the children have a solid foundation of knowledge, understanding and skills before embarking on the more challenging Year 6 work. If the children have worked from the scheme for at least a year, but *you* are not a musician and are new to it, you will need to take time to study the set lessons for Years 3, 4, and 5 to get a clear understanding of the work covered.

How is this scheme different from any other?

The main principal of the three books in this scheme is to produce a comprehensive, enjoyable music curriculum that sets high standards and has high expectations. The feedback from teachers who have used the Foundation and KS1 courses is that Year 1 and 2 children have developed their musical skills markedly. One teacher said her Year 1 children were now matching the skills of Year 5 children who had not at that time started the course.

The five step-by-step lessons at the beginning of each of the four academic years should give you the idea of how music lessons ought to be balanced both in the short-term and in the medium-term. I know from the non-specialists I've talked to that to see headings such as 'Unit 4: Texture' and 'Unit 9: Exploring melody lines' and 'Unit 11: Composing' is baffling. This is because splitting the work into units with meaningless headings fails to offer an overview for the subject, but also means that teachers are not incorporating important elements, such as composing, into their lessons regularly.

Where do we get hold of the 'listening' music?

The QCA programme of study for music states that children should listen to 'a range of live and recorded music from different times and cultures'. You will probably know that it can be difficult to engage children with music that doesn't have a definite beat throughout, and no words! In the Mix and Match section (page 63) I have therefore set out various ways of introducing music that are stimulating and definitely not boring! A few pieces are included on the CDs that accompany the course, but I have made sure that any other recommended pieces can be easily obtained from a CD shop or online, and might well be included in a compilation album, which is the cheapest way of buying such music. My suggestion is that you study the list and just buy the pieces for which your budget allows. The pieces which are integrated into the set lessons, and which you will therefore need to have, are:

'Russian Dance' from *The Nutcracker Suite* by Pyotr Ilyich Tchaikovsky (Year 3)
Sleigh Ride K605, No. 3 by Wolfgang Amadeus Mozart (Year 4)
Baby Elephant Walk by Henry Mancini (Year 5)
Celebration Overture by Philip Lane (Year 6)

All you need to know – a quick revision of the National Curriculum!

1. What is PULSE?

Start clapping now … Make sure your claps are evenly spaced. You have created a **pulse**. Clap more slowly but still with regular time spaces between each clap. Now you are clapping a slower pulse. Then try clapping a quicker pulse. A pulse is simply that!

2. What is BEAT?

Each one of those evenly spaced claps is a **beat**. You can also say 'Keep to the beat' which is another way of saying 'Keep to the pulse' (just to confuse you!)

3. What is TEMPO?

Tempo is the speed at which you are playing or singing. You can play or sing at a slower or faster tempo.

4. What is METRE?

Choose any speed and start clapping evenly again. Now keep clapping at the same speed but clap 1 2 3 repeatedly as you clap and make each first clap louder than the second and third. Don't make the mistake of clapping a longer beat for beat three than for numbers one and two. Your third beat should lead straight back to the next first beat. Now you have a **metre**. You are clapping in 3-time. Change your counting to go up to 4 each time and make sure the first clap is louder than the second, third and fourth. Now you are clapping in 4-time. This is the most commonly used metre and so is often called 'Common Time'. You will have often heard the expression 'Keep in time'. It means keep on the beat or keep a steady pulse as you play or sing. Remember that your pupils might not know what you mean when you first use this expression!

5. What is RHYTHM?

Clap *Happy Birthday to You*. You are doing more than just clapping a pulse or a metre. You are arranging claps of different speeds into a pattern. This pattern is a **rhythm**. In another sense you can also say 'She's got a good sense of rhythm' which means she clearly feels the pulse, the beat, the metre, the general flow of the music and is interpreting it accurately.

6. What is PITCH?

Sing *Happy Birthday to You*. You are singing higher and lower notes i.e. notes of different **pitch**. This particular pattern of pitched notes combined with the rhythmic pattern is the composition for the song *Happy Birthday to you*. You will have heard people say 'It wasn't in tune'. This obviously means that the notes needed to make a particular tune were not being accurately pitched by the singer.

7. What is TIMBRE?

Timbre simply means the quality of a musical sound. Claves have a wooden clacking timbre, drums a thuddy deeper timbre and bells a high, tinkling timbre etc.

8. What are DYNAMICS?

Dynamics is the musical term for how loudly or quietly you sing or play.

9. What are the ELEMENTS (as seen in the National Curriculum)?

All those technical terms above e.g. pitch, timbre, dynamics are **elements**, which are the ingredients of music.

10. What is SOL-FA?

This is the name for a definite pattern of pitched notes that you may well have heard sung in *The Sound of Music* – DO, RE, MI, FA, SO, LA, TI, DO. No matter whether you choose to start on a low note, medium note or high note, if you sing from DO to the higher DO, your voice will respond to your instinctive 'western ear' and come out with the same definite pitched spacing of these sounds. You may think you are simply moving up step by step as you sing each note, but actually the steps between MI and FA and TI and DO are smaller than the others. Don't worry about that, it's just quite interesting! Each of the sounds DO, RE etc. has a hand sign. At the back of the book and on the ECD you will find the Hand Signs chart.

Planning

Long term planning

The most important thing to consider is that you are developing a set of principals which in turn will develop the children's skills, and allow them to grasp concepts easily, learn to read music and really enjoy the music in their lives, whatever form that should take. I look back to my own music lessons until GCSE and remember them as a time to muck around. There seemed to be no control, a great deal of noise and I certainly didn't learn anything, though I did enjoy some of the songs. In my research for this book I have spoken to many music teachers (specialist and non-specialist) and watched them teach. I've also spoken to many children, and the overwhelming feeling is that music in class should be as organised and controlled as possible in order to gain the maximum from the lesson.

In trains and other public places I regularly come upon people using up more than their fair share of 'sound space'. To me, a person on the train talking loudly to someone on a phone so that people at the far end of the carriage can hear what is said, are doing the oral equivalent of scattering their bags over the whole carriage. There is no way that the latter would be tolerated and yet the former is a given nowadays. Parents often talk 'publicly' to their children on trains and the children respond in equally loud voices. So the insensitivity bug is born and sound violation perpetuated. Now we must turn the tide of insensitivity and encourage alertness and sensitivity, and music lessons are a great place to start! This is the only long term planning you need!

Medium-term planning

The five lesson plans for the first half term of each of the four academic years can be regarded as medium-term plans. On the page before each set of five lessons you will see an overview of those five lessons with the headings: **Theme, Music to listen to, Concepts, Medium-term objectives, Song, Resources, Additional Resources**.

In Chapter 5 (page 56) you will find considerable help with putting together your own medium-term plans, including a thorough explanation of how to weave strands from the various headings of the Mix and Match section into your lessons.

Short-term planning

I regard the short-term plan to be one lesson. I consider half an hour a little short and an hour a little long for a KS2 music lesson. Each of the set lesson plans in this book is therefore intended to be approximately forty-five minutes in length. If your school works in units of half an hour or an hour, it doesn't matter if you go on and do a part of the following lesson or if you don't get through the whole lesson, provided you ensure you maintain a breadth and balance of activities. The five set lessons should work out as half a term's work. There are just two headings: **Objectives** and **Additional Resources**. As you will see from Lesson 1, it is understood that you will always have to hand: percussion instruments, a large set of notation cards (which you should cut out from the back of the book or print out from the ECD, stick on card and laminate), the course CD and a whiteboard or blackboard.

Using percussion instruments

Be very strict right from the word go about making sure that children do not automatically, mindlessly start 'twiddling' their instrument before the activity or piece of music has started properly. Apart from the time-wasting element, you're also inadvertently fostering the insensitivity bug, mentioned earlier. This means that children's 'listening' skills are impaired simply because they become used to habitual background noise.

Percussion instruments can be divided into two categories – **pitched** and **non-pitched**.
- **Pitched** simply means that the instrument can produce two different notes – like a xylophone or a glockenspiel that can go up and down, making higher and lower notes.
- **Non-pitched** are those which cannot make higher and lower notes, like a drum, a tambourine or a shaker. You can simply play a beat and a rhythm on these instruments.

Below is a list of required percussion instruments. Don't worry if your funds won't stretch to all those instruments instantly. If six pairs of claves, for example, are needed in a lesson, use any six wooden sounds; if six hand drums are needed, use skinned tambourines to supplement the numbers. As long as you are working with similar sounds within a group, that is fine.

Non-pitched, mainly used for rhythmic work
- 6 small, skinned tambourines
- 6 hand drums with beaters
- 6 maracas or shakers
- 6 pairs of claves (cylindrical sticks which can be tapped together)
- 6 finger cymbals or Indian bells
- 4 guiros
- 4 single-sound woodblocks (a block of wood tapped with a wooden beater)

Non-pitched, mainly used for creative work
- A cabasa
- Bongo drums
- Tam tams
- A chatterbox
- A cowbell
- A rainmaker
- A flexatone
- A metal guiro
- A bamboo scraper
- A double-sound woodblock
- A large skinless tambourine
- A cymbal with a soft beater
- Sleigh bells
- Any other interesting sounds, including from homemade instruments. (Children can be very inventive: creating stringed instruments, stretching rubber bands over cake tins, creating a multitude of different shaker sounds, using an old metal grill with a tea strainer etc.)

Pitched instruments
- A minimum of four of any combination of the following:
    1) metallaphones (metal bars – the more notes, the better)
    2) glockenspiels (metal bars – the more notes, the better)
    3) xylophones (wooden bars – the more notes, the better)
    4) a complete octave (C – C) of chime bars (These are like the individual bars of a metallaphone)

Chapter 1
Year 3 – Five Lesson Plans

Overview of the five lessons – Medium-term plan

Theme: The Beat

Music to listen to:
- 'Russian Dance' from *The Nutcracker Suite* by Tchaikovsky

Concepts:
- Note values
- Beats
- Rhythm
- Canon
- Metre
- Accents
- Rhythmic notation
- Pitch
- Improvisation
- Composition

Medium-term objectives:
- To develop rhythmic skills, working with different metres – 2-time, 3-time and 4-time, and to understand how to build rhythms
- To learn about note values and beats, including the crotchet rest, and get used to working with them
- To develop listening, looking and concentration skills
- To develop pitch sense, working with the sol-fa system and singing a song
- To start to improvise and compose
- To get to know a piece of classical music by Tchaikovsky

Song: *Chop Chop!*

Resources:
- The course CD
- Non-pitched percussion instruments (see the requirement list in the introduction)
- A whiteboard or blackboard
- A set of notation cards, which you should make from the templates at the back of this book or the ECD. You'll need six semibreves o, ten minims ♩, sixteen crotchets ♩, sixteen pairs of quavers ♫ and four crotchet rests ♪
- Lyrics of the song *Chop Chop!*
- Photocopiables/print-outs as required (see individual lesson plan)

Additional Resources:
- A pitched instrument such as a glockenspiel or metallaphone
- CD of 'Russian Dance' from *The Nutcracker Suite* by Tchaikovsky
- Several small empty plastic water bottles

Lesson 1

If you are not a music specialist you will need to have read the introduction to the book before starting on the first lesson. Don't be alarmed by the length of these five set lesson plans. The actual lesson is approximately forty-five minutes in length. The explanation is to help you teach effectively. Many concepts are introduced in these five lessons. Don't worry if the children don't have much depth of understanding at this stage. You have the rest of the academic year to really work with these concepts and develop their integral skills.

Objectives:
- To get used to working with four different note values – **quavers**, **crotchets**, **minims**, **semibreves** – focusing on keeping in time
- To learn a new song – *Chop Chop!*
- To understand how rhythm and beat help with moving to music effectively
- To become familiar with 'Russian Dance' from *The Nutcracker Suite* by *Tchaikovsky*

Additional Resources:
- CD tracks 1 and 2. From now on the CD should always be at hand.
- Whiteboard or Blackboard. From now on this should always be at hand.
- **Crotchet, minim, quavers, semibreve** notation cards.
- Lyrics of the song *Chop Chop!*
- CD of 'Russian Dance' from *The Nutcracker Suite* by Tchaikovsky

Listen to the beat! (working with 4 different beats)
- Tell the children they are going to listen carefully to the CD (track 1) to try and notice how many different **speeds of beat** they can hear. They are also listening out for lower notes and higher notes. Is there any pattern to this? So sit and listen in silence until the track is finished and then talk about what you heard. (The children should have heard four different speeds of beat, and they may have noticed that there were alternate sections of lower and higher notes, of equal length.)
- Play the track again. This time join in clapping with each section of lower notes, and clapping very quietly with each section of higher notes. Concentrate hard to see if you can all recall the order of the speeds when you talk about it at the end: 1) medium 2) slow 3) medium 4) fast 5) medium 6) very slow 7) medium

Understanding how the beats fit into each other
- For those of you who haven't covered the KS1 scheme, you need to know the musical names for the different notes and their varying speeds of beat. If we are being technically correct these are not actually speeds but **durations** of time. This will become clear at the end of this lesson; don't worry about it for now. Hold up the four different notation cards which show the four different beats that you heard on the CD.

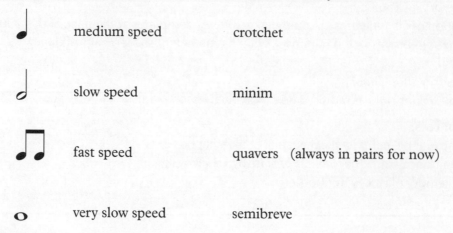

- Spend some time checking that the children are certain of the names of the notes, their relative speeds and their musical symbols. Have they thoroughly grasped that two quavers fit into one crotchet, two crotchets fit into one minim, two minims fit into one semibreve? Check out the diagram below. You might like to write it up on the board and/or write some 'musical sums' on the board for the children to do. There are three examples below:

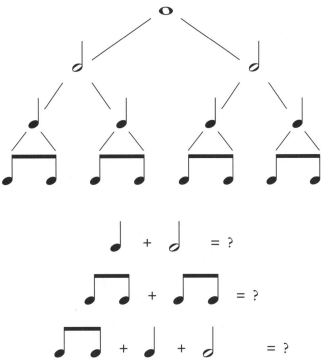

- Listen carefully to track 2 of the CD and see if you can hear all four of the different beats being played at the same time.

Stepping and clapping round the room

- Get ready to walk round the room. With track 1 take eight medium-paced steps for the first **phrase** (or musical sentence) then stand still and clap gently at that same speed for the higher phrase. Continue like this for the rest of the track, matching your speed of footsteps with the beat for each lower phrase, and standing still to clap each higher phrase.
- Half the class should do the walking while the other half appraise, then swap. Discuss which children were anticipating the change of beat so managed to change their steps to fit the new beat at exactly the right moment.

Singing *Chop Chop!*

- Start to learn the song *Chop Chop!* using the lyrics provided. Alternatively this particular song is quite easy to learn by rote, with the help of a few key words written on the board. CD track 3 has the vocal line to help you. It's up to you how to facilitate the learning process. With a song like this it works well to play right through the song on the CD while encouraging the children to join in with the chorus. At the same time they will be grasping the slightly more complex verses. With other songs you might like to use the pause button on the remote so the children can copy a section at a time. We will be re-visiting this song in the next two lessons so don't feel you have to learn it completely here. This 'gradual' learning should apply to all songs in the book.

Introducing a piece of classical music – 'Russian Dance' from *The Nutcracker Suite* by Tchaikovsky

- First listen to the music on your CD (it's only sixty seconds long!). As you listen, try clapping to the music's obvious quick beat (NB always do small claps for a quick beat). When everyone is secure with that, after around half a minute, lead the children into clapping a beat that is twice as slow. When they are secure with that, lead them into a beat that is twice as slow as *that*.
- Play the track again and repeat the three different speeds of clapping, to help develop the children's all-important 'inner pulse'.

Working out actions to go with 'Russian Dance'

- For now just get used to the following three simple actions. Practise them with the music, in any order, changing from one to another whenever you want.

1. To the obvious faster beat, do on-the-spot jumps from foot to foot in time with the music, kicking each foot forwards.
2. To the obvious slower beat:
   a) Stretch right arm up and look up
   b) Return to static position
   c) Stretch left arm up and look up
   d) Return to static position

Set choreography

Having fun improvising

3. Also to the obvious slower beat and from the same static position as for the previous action, step to the right and join the other foot in a stamp, then repeat to the left.

Passing claps round the circle

1. Four crotchets each

- It's great to use a piece of pop music with a strong beat as a backing track for this activity, though carefully chosen short pieces of classical music to which you can clap a steady beat will also work. The most important factor is to be able to count naturally in fours to the chosen music The children should sit in a circle and 'pass' a clapped beat around, coming in at the right moment and maintaining the beat at precisely the established speed

- First try clapping four crotchets each. Begin by counting to 4 at a steady, medium walking pace. The first child should then start clapping, keeping to this exact speed. (This is sometimes referred to as 'bringing them in'.) When everyone has clapped four crotchets each, without a break, send the claps round the circle again but this time only clap two each; then without a break send just one round each. There is no definitive **tempo** (speed) for a crotchet; according to the music your tempo might be on the slightly slow or the slightly quick side of medium. *You* should stand in the middle of the circle looking at the child whose turn it is next, to keep everyone on their toes!

2. Semibreves

- Each child claps a **semibreve** – clap on beat 1 and then keep the hands together and 'pulse' them for beats 2, 3 and 4. Imagine that each clap is a pair of finger cymbals being played and the 'pulses' are the finger chimes ringing on. Make sure you do not cut short beats 2, 3 and 4 or you are not clapping the full length of a **semibreve**. (Earlier in this lesson I explained that the speed of the beat is really a **duration** of time. This statement probably makes more sense in the context of clapping **semibreves** here. A **semibreve** lasts for four beats, a crotchet, for one beat, a minim for two beats and a pair of quavers for one beat.)

3. Alternate semibreves and crotchets

- As above, but this time the children should alternate: 1) 4 crotchets 2) a semibreve 3) 4 crotchets, and so on.

Lesson 2

Objectives:

- To play percussion from notated music
- To play in canon
- To understand the difference between a beat and a rhythm, and to develop rhythmic skills

Additional Resources:

- Four pairs of claves, four hand drums (or any two sets of percussion instruments with contrasting sounds). From now on percussion instruments should always be on hand.
- Lyrics of the song *Chop Chop!*

Stepping and clapping

- Do the *Stepping and clapping* sequence from Lesson 1 with the CD (track 1).

How the notes look when written down (or notated)

- Sit down and play track 1 of the CD again. Memorise the order of the notes in the sequence – **crotchets, minims, crotchets, quavers, crotchets, semibreves, crotchets** – with the children. Look again at these four different types of notes on notation cards. Try holding up a card and choosing a reliable pupil to clap the beat shown. The others should join in when the child has established the **beat**.
- Copy the sequence below on to the board. This emulates the CD but with each phrase reduced in length. Ask the children to sit and clap it through as you point to each note. Can they follow it just as well if you don't point?

- This is the correct way to notate music. The vertical lines are called **bar lines**, which separate the notes into **bars**. In each bar the notes add up to **four crotchet counts** or **beats**.

Playing the piece above on percussion instruments

- First establish the zero tolerance 'no twiddling' rules for percussion instruments (see *Introduction*). As long as this rule is being observed, make sure you then zap straight into the activity so the children realise it is worthwhile concentrating on keeping their hands away from the instruments initially in order to subsequently have much more playing time.
- Give pairs of claves to four children and hand drums and beaters to four other children (or any two sets of instruments with contrasting sounds). The remaining children will be responsible for watching and listening to the instruments being played, ready to appraise what they saw and heard afterwards.
- The children playing claves play the sequence on the board, keeping perfectly in time. (Don't forget to count them in by counting to 4 at the pace they will then play their crotchets.) Point to each note to guide them. The children playing hand drums then do the same. This might seem simple stuff but it is important to establish rules that will engender high personal expectations of the children's musical performance.
- Now the two groups are going to play the piece in **canon** (a round). They will have to follow the notes with their eyes, rather than your guiding finger. The claves start first, then after the first four crotchets the drums start.
- Divide the rest of the class into groups so they can play the piece in canon in the same way. Appraise each performance and depending on the level of accuracy, repeat the activity if necessary.

Understanding the difference between a beat and a rhythm

- If you just clap continuous crotchets, you are clapping a **beat**. If you mix up different types of notes – crotchets, quavers etc – you are clapping a **rhythm**.
- Remembering that you must have **the equivalent of four crotchet beats in one bar**, make adjustments to what you have written on the board. Use the example below if you want, or create your own piece. In our example we have cut out the last four bars so the piece is only four bars long. We have altered beats 3 and 4 in the first bar, beats 1 and 2 in the second bar, beats 1 and 2 in the third bar and all four beats in the fourth bar. Your own adjustments might be different from this.
- Try clapping your new version. You might need more than one attempt!

Chop Chop!

- First sing through the song with the CD. Either use track 3, joining in with the vocals, or sing to the accompaniment (track 4).
- Now add an instrumental accompaniment of your choice.
- The instruments in the plan below have been chosen for their 'clean', short sounds, in the case of the crotchets and quavers, and for their ability to sustain a longer ringing sound in the case of the minims and semibreves, emphasizing the fact that beats are **durations** of sound. Choose different instruments if you want but bear these points in mind. Divide the class into ten groups. Group 8 and group 10 have a **rhythm** to play. The other groups all have a **beat**. Remember that everybody should still be singing!

Group 1:   Chorus 1   – crotchets   – woodblocks

Group 2:   Verse 1   – minims   – finger cymbals

Group 3:   Chorus 2   – crotchets   – tambourines

Group 4:   Verse 2   – quavers   – claves

Group 5:   Chorus 3   – crotchets   – sandblocks

Group 6:   Verse 3   – semibreves   – cymbals

Group 7:   Chorus 4   – crotchets   – hand drums

Group 8:   Verse 4   –   – woodblocks

Group 9:   Chorus 5   – crotchets   – tambourines

Group 10:   Verse 5   –   – claves

All groups: Chorus 6   – crotchets   – all instruments

'Russian Dance' with actions

- If you have time, finish with listening to this while randomly executing the actions learnt in Lesson 1.

Lesson 3

Objectives:

- To introduce **metre** and **accent**
- To learn about **phrasing** and **structure** through a choreographed piece
- To introduce **pitch**

Additional Resources:

- CD of 'Russian Dance' from *The Nutcracker Suite* by Tchaikovsky
- A glockenspiel or another **pitched** percussion instrument
- Copy of the *Hand Signs* sheet
- Lyrics of the song *Chop Chop!*

Stepping and clapping

- Warm up with this activity.

Analysing the music of 'Russian Dance' and choreographing an action piece

- Listen to the music on the CD, but this time only clap the *fast* beat while counting quietly and repeatedly up to eight throughout the track. Every time you and the children complete a set of eight counts, put a mark on the board. See how many marks you have made by the end (you have to be ready to start counting the very second the music starts!). These twenty-one sections are called **phrases** (musical sentences). Listening out for phrases in a piece of music is a good way to work out the **structure** of the whole piece. Some **phrases** have the same tune or general style or 'feel' as others. This can help to decide which actions should accompany which parts of the piece.
- Remind yourselves of the three different actions you tried out last time.
- Now plan with the children which of those actions to do for which part of the music. Don't make it too complicated. Name the actions 1, 2 and 3, and put one of those numbers beside each of your marks on the board as you all listen to the music again. Keep it simple. You might start by alternating two of the actions for the first **eight** lots of eight beats, and then when there is an obvious change in the music, introduce the third action, and so on.

Sol-fa pitched notes

- First check that the children understand what pitch is. Clap the rhythm of any song e.g. *Happy Birthday to You* and see if the children can recognise it. Explain that had you sung it through to 'la', even without words they would have recognised it because of the tune – effectively a pattern of pitched notes. You will be singing *at a lower or higher pitch*, according to whether you start the song on a low note or a high one.
- In KS1 we introduced pitch with body shapes. Here we are going to build on that work. First practise the shapes from lowest to highest in the photograph. The children should do this in a space of their own in time with your playing of notes from C to High C on the glockenspiel or metallaphone. Play each note four times, bouncing the beater on the centre of each bar to give a reasonable length of time to remain in one shape before moving up to the next.

- Explain that we are going to call these notes by **sol-fa** names. **Sol-fa** is simply the name of a system to help you to sing in tune. Play each note on your glockenspiel from **C** to **High C** again and all sing **do, ré, mi, fa, so, la, ti, do** (as in *The Sound of Music*) as you play each note.

Hand Signs

- Show the hand signs **do**, **mi** and **so** from the photocopiable sheet/ECD and try to learn them.
- The children should sit up straight, cross-legged but relaxed with hands in laps. This gives a feeling of concentration and of readiness to listen. They are going to imitate the exact sounds they hear. Track 5 of the CD comprises four sets of eight sequences of **sol-fa** notes. Each sequence is followed by a precise time space in which to copy it. It is just the first set that should be copied here. The only notes used are **do, mi, so** and **high do**, and each of the little sequences comprises three or four notes. When you all echo them, also show the hand sign for each sound. For **high do** simply do the same hand sign as for the lower **do**, but hold your fist a little higher.

Accents and Metre

- Tell the children to clap whatever you play, and also to notice *what* you are playing, ready to comment at the end. Remind them of the difference between a **rhythm** and a **beat**.
- First play a hand drum at a regular **crotchet pulse**. After this is established, make the first of every four taps louder than the others. You are making an **accent** to show **4-time**. Go back to playing regular beats with no **accents**. When this is established, introduce an **accent** on every first one of three beats to show **3-time**. Go back to playing regular beats with no accents. When this is established, introduce an **accent** on the first of every two beats to show **2-time**.
- Can the children say what you did? (You played in 4s, then in 3s, then in 2s.)

Metre making

- Now the children should walk round the room (or walk on the spot if there isn't enough room!) in time to your steady **crotchet pulse** on the drum, and only clap on the **accented** first of each four beats to show **4-time**. This can also be described as showing a **4-time metre**.
- Try the same exercise in a **3-time metre** and in a **2-time metre**.
- Try changing from one **metre** to another without warning and see how quickly the children can adjust their clapping pattern.

Chop Chop!

- Finish off with a sing-through of this song with or without percussion accompaniment. Can the children tell you what **metre** the song is in?

Lesson 4

Objectives:
- To mix **metres**
- To **internalise** beats
- To develop **pitch** sense
- To introduce **improvisation**

Additional Resources:
- Eight plastic water bottles each containing about five centimetres of water (to weight them)

Bash the bottle!
- This new warm-up activity is a variation of *Passing claps round the circle* from Lesson 1.
- The class should sit in a circle. Eight random children have a bottle in front of them. Each child with a bottle is going to 'do' four **crotchet beats**. On the first beat they lift the bottles in the air, on the second and third beats they tap them on the floor in front of themselves and on the fourth beat they tap them on the floor in front of the child to their left. Continue passing the bottles round to this precise beat, taking care that the bottle stays upright. When you have just passed a bottle, look out for the next one coming!

Metre making
- Revise this activity from the last lesson.

Mixing metres
- Divide the class into two equal groups. *You* are going to maintain a lightly tapped crotchet pulse on a drum, while both groups carry out the following instructions at the same time. Group 1 should shout 'Hey!' on the first of each of three crotchet beats, and gently clap the other two, making a **3-time metre**. Group 2 should do the same in a **4-time metre** as shown. All children should quietly say the numbers out loud as well as clapping. The 'Hey!' will only coincide every twelve beats. See the illustration below, which shows the first twelve beats. Keep going for as long as you like.

Group 1:	Hey!	2	3	Hey!	2	3	Hey!	2	3	Hey!	2	3
Group 2:	Hey!	2	3	4	Hey!	2	3	4	Hey!	2	3	4

- Now try it without the claps. The children should count in their heads as you play the drum pulse even more lightly. It is worth developing this skill of maintaining a steady pulse without vocalising. The children are then **internalising** the pulse. Finally don't play the pulse on the drum at all. Simply count the children in, and then they are on their own!

The Pitch Game
- This was introduced in the KS1 book and will be extended here. On track 6 of the CD there are some very short extracts of music, each of which ends on do, mi, so or high do. Allocate places in the room for each of these four pitches. The children should listen to the extracts and when you press the pause button at the end of each one they should hum the last note, trying to work out what it is, then go to the appropriate allocated place, according to what they think it is. Those children who go to the correct place are still 'in' and can remain standing for the next extract, while those children who were wrong should sit down. (The answers are below.) Just do the first five examples in this lesson.

1	do		6	mi
2	so		7	do
3	mi		8	high do
4	high do		9	so
5	so		10	so

(The last five are covered in the *Mix and Match* section page 63 but the answers are given here in case you are feeling enthusiastic!)

Improvisation and Composition – what's the difference?

- An **improvisation** is something that is played, sung or spoken and if it were to be repeated, would not come out exactly the same the second time. It's a spontaneous, unrehearsed piece. A **composition** is a *learnt* piece which, allowing for interpretation, will always come out sounding the same. A **composition** can be created from an **improvisation** and then written down *or* can be written down first and then played.

An improvisation based on the song *Chop Chop!*

- You will see from the *Mix and Match* section that it is possible to inspire composition and improvisation in many ways – through a poem, a picture, a story, a theme or a piece of existing music as well as using a rhythmic pattern as the starting point. Here we are taking the song *Chop Chop!* and developing an improvisation, which simply means we are exploring ideas for sounds and seeing what we come up with. Even with an improvisation it is useful to have some discussion beforehand to consider what will be musically effective.

- So, sit in a circle with all the instruments in the middle and consider ...

  1. ... **whether the improvisation will have a beat to it**. It's probably a good idea to have a beat because that will capture the nature of the song with the woodcutter's chops at the heart of the piece.

  2. ... **any interesting rhythms**. Try clapping the words 'chop chop' followed by two silent beats, and repeat these four beats a few times. Maybe this would make a good rhythmic 'motif' to be a feature of the piece. This can then dictate the beat throughout, to be observed by all players.

  3. ... **what instruments to use and how to play them**. How about wooden sounds to represent the chopping of the wood and branches creaking? Shaker sounds might represent leaves rustling in the woods. Birds flying away might be conveyed by sliding the beater up a glockenspiel or xylophone, or both. What about rabbits hopping, or the wolf creeping away? All these might inspire different sounds (**timbre**) and different ways of playing. As long as everyone's contribution fits the main beat set by the words 'chop chop' followed by the two beats of silence, then the piece will work.

  4. ... **when to play**. Remember there are no constraints. You don't have to play the birds flying away, followed by the mice etc. in the same order as in the song. You might prefer to simply create the atmosphere of the words of the song, so the sounds that the listener will hear convey the general atmosphere of the woods. On the other hand, it might be a good way of organising the piece to have the various creatures appearing in the same order as in the song. It's up to you.

  5. ... **how to create interest**. It is great to have contrast in musical pieces – moments when the texture of the music is thin (fewer instruments playing) and when it is thick (more instruments playing), times when there might be a solo or even a short silence, moments which are loud or quiet (**dynamics**) or fast or slow. If, for example, three children are conveying the mice scurrying away with fast quiet sounds on guiros and another three are conveying the squirrels scampering away with similar sounds on cabasas, and no-one else is playing for a few seconds (apart from maybe the 'chop chop' motif), then this would be a great contrast to, say, a single quiet drum thud representing the wolf creeping away at the end.

  6. ... **who is going to play what instrument**. For this first piece it is probably best to assign instruments to children yourself.

  7. ... **how long the piece should be**. A minute is a good length of time for a piece such as this. To get the feel of a minute as a time frame, all stand up and while *you* keep track of the seconds, the children should be 'feeling' the length of the minute by counting to sixty at what they perceive to be in seconds. At the end of what they *think* is a minute they should sit down. Who was the most accurate?

  8. Now go for it!

Lesson 5

Objectives:
- To introduce the **crotchet rest**
- To turn an improvisation into a composition
- To continue to work on rhythm and pitch

Additional Resources:
- Plastic water bottles
- The notation card showing a crotchet rest
- Copies of the *Rhythm Patterns 1* sheet

Bash the bottle!
- Start with this warm-up activity.
- Try it in **3-time**, so each child does only *one* tap in front of him- or her-self.
- Try with more bottles.

Introducing the crotchet rest
- A **rest** is a short period of silence, and in music silence is just as important as sound. The **crotchet rest** is worth exactly **one crotchet beat of silence**. Show the children the notation card.
- Write the following four patterns of **crotchets** and **rests** on the board:

- Count the children in (four counts) then simply clap each pattern four times, going on to the next pattern without a break. Show the **rest** by turning palms up.
- Try this again but clap each pattern twice. Finally clap each pattern just once.
- Can the children remember the sequence without looking at the board i.e. clapping each pattern four times, then twice, then once? Try clapping the whole sequence by heart. This requires concentration, rhythmic precision and forward thinking.

Turning the improvisation *Chop Chop!* into a composition
- Remind yourselves of the elements that made up your *Chop Chop!* improvisation in the last lesson and try playing it through again.
- Discuss how closely it resembled your previous version and how to refine it so it becomes more of a set composition, rather than something you are making up as you go along.
- As a class you need to agree on a format for your piece then *you* write the ideas on the board in order, in the form of brief instructions. You should then 'conduct' the piece yourself, either signalling to the various groups to stop/start/continue while tapping the air to show the beat, or point to the board so that the children can follow the directions to see when it is their turn.
- In Year 4, **graphic scores** will be introduced so you can learn to write down compositions such as this and also how to interpret **graphic scores** in order to play compositions.

Pitch echoes
- In a moment you will choose a child to imitate what *you* played on a pitched percussion instrument, such as a glockenspiel.
- You and the children need to know that **mi = E** and **so = G**. Play the first example that follows on the glockenspiel, following the rhythm as well as the pitch. The children must listen but not look then the chosen child should try to play exactly what you played. Was it correct? Ask the class.

- Move on to the next example with a different child and continue in this way. In the six examples that follow, **m = mi (E)** and **s = so (G)**

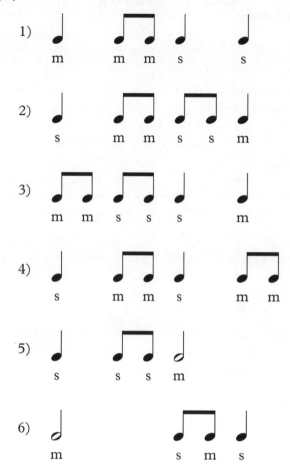

Hear the rhythm, see the rhythm

- Two skills are being developed in this activity – matching up the *sound* of a rhythm with the *sight* of that rhythm, and recognising combinations of two different pitches.
- Give out copies of the *Rhythm Patterns 1* sheet. The children can work alone or in pairs for this activity. Keep a sheet for yourself which you have filled in in advance to show the order of the examples you intend to play, as well as an indication of which **sol-fa** notes you intend to play, e.g. for the fifth rhythm on the sheet

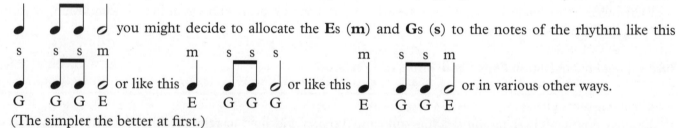

(The simpler the better at first.)

- Ask the children to write the number 1, 2 etc. beside each respective rhythm to indicate the order in which they think you played the rhythms, and if possible write 's' or 'm' above each note of the rhythm to indicate whether they think it is a **so** or a **mi**. You might have to play each example two or three times. Alternatively, if the children find this difficult, they can simply work out the order first. Check the answers with them before going on to attempt the pitches.

From here, go to Chapter 5 (page 56) for help with devising your own lesson plans from the various headings in Chapter 6 (page 63). Good luck!

Chapter 2
Year 4 – Five Lesson Plans

Overview of the five lessons – Medium-term plan

Theme: Transport, and being transported!

Music to listen to: *Sleigh Ride* K605, No. 3 by Mozart

Concepts:
- Graphic scores
- Instruments of the orchestra
- Structure
- Ostinato

Medium-term objectives:
- To learn how to devise and interpret **graphic scores**
- To learn about the instruments of the **orchestra**
- To develop **pitch** sense
- To develop rhythmic sense and to learn a new note value – the **dotted minim** $\rlap{\,.}{\downharpoonleft}$
- To extend knowledge of music from different times and cultures
- To develop group composing skills
- To improve singing and instrumental playing technique

Song: *Magic Carpet*

Resources:
- Course CD
- Whiteboard/blackboard
- Percussion instruments
- Lyrics to the song *Magic Carpet*

Additional Resources:
- CD of *Sleigh Ride* K605, No. 3 by Mozart
- Photocopiables/print-outs as needed (see individual lesson plans)
- Pieces of card (see Lesson 1)

Lesson 1

If the children are new to this scheme of work so haven't worked through the set lesson plans for Year 3, it is essential that you do that now before embarking on the lessons that follow. It might take you less than half a term to get through the five lessons, but it is important that you and the children have a solid foundation of knowledge, understanding and skills before embarking on this more challenging Year 4 work.

If the children worked from the scheme last year, but you are not a musician and are new to the scheme, you will need to take time to study the set lessons for Year 3 to get a clear understanding of the work covered.

Objectives:
- To develop the skill of 'scan' listening
- To introduce **graphic scores**
- To listen to *Sleigh Ride* K605, No. 3 by Mozart
- To improve rhythmic skills, working in 3-time
- To learn a new song – *Magic Carpet*

Additional Resources:
- Small pieces of card for 'Animal Ark' (see below)
- Photocopies/print-outs of the graphic score *Dustman's Drudge*
- CD of *Sleigh Ride* K605, No. 3 by Mozart
- **Dotted minim** notation card
- Lyrics of the song *Magic Carpet*

Animal Ark
- This is a great listening activity to warm up the ears! Decide whether you want to play the game in pairs or threes according to the numbers in your class.
- In a class of twenty you will need to think of ten different animals/birds that make a distinctive noise. Here are ten ideas: Mouse, cat, dog, sheep, cow, horse, donkey, duck, hen, frog.
- For twenty children you'll need twenty small cards. On two of them write the word 'mouse'. On two of them write 'cat' etc. Shuffle the cards and give them out. The children must remember what is on their card and return the cards to you.
- They then sit (if space allows) or stand as far apart as possible, all facing in different directions. At a given signal they start to make the relevant animal noise quite loudly while listening out for someone else making the same noise. Only when a child hears someone else making the *same* sound can they go and sit/stand with that child and both children then stop making the sound. If a child goes to another child whom he *thought* was making the same sound and finds that, in fact he was mistaken, that's tough. He must stay there!
- This game encourages 'scan listening' where the children are trying to identify a specific sound from a whole array of sounds. In a larger class adapt the game (unless you can think of enough distinctive noises!) so that you might have three children each with the same animal/bird sound. Alternatively divide the class into two. One half plays the game, the other half observes, then swap.

Introducing graphic scores to record (write down) a composition
- Write this poem up on the board. Listen to the poem on track 7 of the CD then play it again but this time join in speaking it out loud:

Dustman's Drudge
Motor turning, motor turning,
Jumping from the van and rushing to the bin.
Heave it high then trudge with the drudgery,
Fix it on the lorry and tip it all in.
Crashing, crunching, grating, munching,
Churning rubbish in a splattertonic spin.

- You are now going to play a composition from a **graphic score**, which shows the class exactly what to play, when.
- Give out copies of the graphic score *Dustman's Drudge* sheet or copy it on to the board. This shows one way that a **graphic score** can be devised to represent this poem.
- As a class, consider the instruments we have chosen to represent the various ideas in the poem, listed down the left of the page. Remember, the purpose of the poem is to inspire the musical composition; there is no need to represent every single word with a sound, nor to represent the exact order of events. The 'splattertonic spin', for example, is conveyed by mixing all the sounds to create a greater density (as you can see from the last ten seconds of the score). The motor of the lorry is turning over all the time, though only just ticking over when the squares are less dense, and probably going along in first gear for the slightly more densely filled squares. So this is simply a sound collage to suggest the Dustman's round. Interpret the symbols as you like. They are there to give you a feel for the volume, the speed and the density of sound.
- Select pupils to play the various instruments/parts outlined in the graphic score.
- When you have had a good discussion about how the members of the group should play to make sure the sound clearly represents the symbols, look at the time frame, indicated across the top of the sheet. Explain to the children that *you* will show the first period of ten seconds by starting with your right arm stretched up beside your right ear then slowly lowering it for the duration of ten seconds – (estimate approximately by counting in your head), and to show the next period of ten seconds you will slowly raise your arm until it is stretched up beside your ear again, and continue like this.
- Now tell the class to get ready. They should be silent, keeping an eye on you as well as looking at the score. Count the children in by counting to four at the approximate pulse of seconds then begin 'conducting', which is the cue for the guiros to start the piece.
- You might like to record your piece and listen back to it.

Listening to a piece of classical music – *Sleigh Ride* K605, No. 3 by Mozart

- This piece is in 3-time (quite fast) but it is not a particularly obvious feeling of 3-time during the first two phrases.
- Stand in a circle and be prepared to stamp on the very first beat of the music. Follow the stamp with two claps and continue like this, stamping on the first of each group of three beats with one foot, then doing two claps, and then stamping with the other foot and doing two claps. (As long as you start with the first beat that you hear, the threes will work out.) When you hear the sleigh bells start, change your actions to finger clicks on the first of each of the three beats, and gentler claps for beats two and three. Go back to the 'stamp, clap, clap' pattern for louder parts of the music, then to the 'click, clap, clap' pattern for the gentler sections.
- Play the music again and do the actions, but this time *you* introduce a third pattern – patting your knees on the first beat and doing two claps on the other two beats. You can change to this action whenever you feel that you've done enough of the 'stamp, clap, clap' actions.

Revising the dotted minim

- This note was first introduced in Year 2.
- First, ask the children to do the 'click, clap, clap' pattern they were doing to *Sleigh Ride* but without the music, while *you* play finger chimes on each click. Notice how the sound rings on during the second and third beats of each set of three beats.
- Tell the children that this is a 3-count note, which has the duration of three crotchets and is called a **dotted minim**. Show the notation card.
- You might like to try the activity *Passing claps round the circle* (taught in Lesson 1 of Year 3, page 12) with every other child clapping three crotchets and every other child, a dotted minim (clap on beat one and pulse hands on beats two and three.)

A new song – *Magic Carpet*

- Listen to this song on the CD, track 8. Notice how it has two different metres. It goes from 4-time to 3-time to 4-time, to 3-time and back to 4-time. You might like to refresh your memory by looking at the activity from Year 3 on page 18.
- Give out copies of the lyrics or view them on the whiteboard/OHP and start to learn the song.

25

Lesson 2

Objectives:

- To create a graphic score
- To develop awareness of how sounds can represent words/create an atmosphere
- To explore the structure of *Sleigh Ride* K605, No. 3 by Mozart
- To learn a new sol-fa note – **ré**

Additional Resources:

- Pieces of card for *Animal Ark*
- Copies of the *Blank graphic score sheet*
- 'Homemade' instruments
- CD of *Sleigh Ride* K605, No. 3 by Mozart
- Lyrics of the song *Magic Carpet*

Animal Ark

- Warm up the ears with a game of this!

Creating a graphic score

- Having played our musical interpretation of the poem *Dustman's Drudge,* you are now going to create your own. (Therefore you are approaching composition the other way round from the '*Chop Chop!*' composition in Year 3, by 'composing' on to paper and then playing what is written down, rather than creating a composition from an improvisation.)
- Copy the poem *Dustman's Drudge* (page 24) on to the board and work together as a class this first time.
- First consider which instruments you want to represent which sounds in the poem. Rather than having the motor ticking over throughout (as in our interpretation) you might decide to have the idea of 'trudge with the drudgery' as something that creates a solid thud in the background throughout. Alternatively, you might want to just focus on creating sounds for the four verbs in line five and the one in line six. Or you might have another idea entirely. (NB This is a great opportunity for bringing in homemade instruments.)
- Next you need to consider the **structure** (shape) of your piece. Discuss which instruments should play when. Don't fill in every square because the music needs to 'breathe,' and do take time to consider how the various instrument combinations will sound.
- Now for the symbols – you can be as creative as you want. These should simply suggest *to you* how the instruments are being played. The denser the square, the more sound is happening and the richer the **texture** of the music; dots are likely to represent **staccato** (very short) sounds, and swirls, smoother sounds. Remember this isn't an exact form of notation like crotchets and quavers etc.
- After plenty of discussion, you might like to roughly draw whatever you come up with on the board, and then give out copies of the *Blank graphic score sheet,* and ask each child to fill one in.
- Finally divide the class into five groups and give out the instruments. Make sure the children are silent and ready to concentrate on their scores, as well as keeping an eye on the time frame that you are indicating with your arm movements. Then after counting them in, go for it!
- You might like to record it and listen to the result.

Exploring the structure of *Sleigh Ride*

- First write up or project the **structure** (below) on the board.
- A represents the first musical idea, B, the second and C, the third.

> **A A A A**
> **B B B B (sleigh bells)**
> **A A**
> **C C (fanfare)**
> **Little sleigh bells joining section (4 lots of 3)**
> **B B A**
> **B A C**
> **Sleigh bells fading out**

- This analysis that we have done, in order to work out the **structure** of the piece, is particularly useful when you want to add percussion instruments or actions to a piece.
- Now play the music and notice how it falls into **phrases** (musical sections) of eight bars – i.e. you can count '1, 2, 3' eight times, and then a new phrase starts. At the asterisks in the analysis, the **B** only lasts for four sets of three beats, and the A, for a further four.
- As the music is playing, *you* point to the letters on the board so you can all get a feel for the **phrasing** and **structure** of the piece. You may well have to listen to the piece twice for this to be clear to you all.

Introducing a new *sol-fa* note – ré
- Firstly you play up the scale from **do** (**C**) to **high do** (**C**) on a pitched instrument so the children can sing the **sol-fa** notes (**do, ré, mi, fa, so, la, ti, do**) and show the hand signs of those they know.
- The new **sol-fa** sound is **ré**, (**D**) which fits between **do** (**C**) and **mi** (**E**). Show the hand sign for **ré**.
- Using track 5 of the CD, try echoing *Set 2* of eight sequences while showing the hand signs. The sound **ré** is included in these examples and some slightly more complex rhythms.

Singing *Magic Carpet*
- Continue to learn the song, with track 8 and/or track 9, which is the accompaniment only.

Lesson 3

Objectives:
- To introduce the instruments of the orchestra and identify their different **timbres**
- To work with the new *sol-fa* note – *ré*
- To add a percussion accompaniment to *Sleigh Ride* K605, No. 3 by Mozart

Additional Resources:
- Sheets of paper and pencils for all
- Copies of the *Rhythm Patterns 2* sheet
- Lyrics of the song *Magic Carpet*
- CD of *Sleigh Ride* K605, No. 3 by Mozart

The orchestra

- Show on the board in a simple diagram like the one below, how the orchestra is put together with four **families** of instruments, and how these **families** are arranged (roughly!) on the concert platform. Below the diagram is a list of the most commonly used instruments from each.

- Listen twice to the CD tracks 10 - 22 to hear short extracts of the orchestral instruments listed above. (The track numbers appear beside each instrument – we haven't included the viola sound here however, as it is difficult for children to discriminate between it and the sound of the violin.) Are the children able to name the instruments, before you tell them, just from listening to the extracts? Talk about their different timbres (quality of sound). Whenever you listen to a piece of music in the future try to identify these timbres.

Woodwind

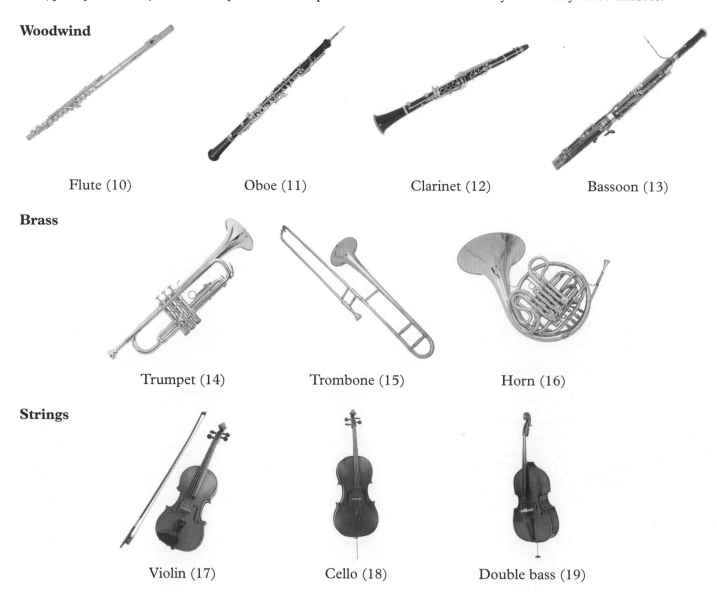

Flute (10) Oboe (11) Clarinet (12) Bassoon (13)

Brass

Trumpet (14) Trombone (15) Horn (16)

Strings

Violin (17) Cello (18) Double bass (19)

Percussion

Bass drum (20)

Kettle drum
or Timpani (21)

Snare drum (22)

- Give out pieces of paper and ask the children to number 1 to 10 down the left-hand side. Play any ten of the thirteen tracks again in a random order. Can the children identify each instrument and write down its name as it is played?

Working in 3-time with the new note *ré*

- In Lesson 5 of the Year 3 set lessons, the activity *Hear the rhythm, see the rhythm* was introduced. We are going to repeat this here, but extend the exercise by including the note **do** and the new note **ré**.
- Give out copies of the *Rhythm Patterns 2* sheet. These rhythms are in 3-time and are two bars long. The children can work alone or in pairs for this activity. Keep a sheet for yourself that you have filled in in advance to show the order of the examples you intend to play (you don't have to do all of them). You might like to just take half a dozen random examples from the sheet. Below are two examples from the sheet (rhythm numbers 3 and 6). You will see that we have kept it very simple.

- When you play one of the rhythms, the children must scan the sheet trying to recognise which *rhythm* it is. At this stage they needn't worry about the sol-fa notes. You might need to play the example two or three times. Ask the children to write the number 1 beside the rhythm on the sheet that they think you played.
- Now play the rhythm again. This time the children are listening for which sol-fa notes you are playing. They should write 's', 'm', 'r' or 'd' above each note of the rhythm to indicate whether they think you played a **so**, a **mi**, a **ré** or a **do**.

A percussion accompaniment to *Sleigh Ride*

- Now you have analysed the **structure** of this piece and got used to the style and 'feel' of the music you are only a step away from joining in with the piece by playing a percussion **accompaniment**.
- Re-write the analysis of the **structure** of the piece from the last lesson on the board.
- Four lots of eight bars is rather a long time to have the same instruments accompanying. Instead, have two different groups of instruments such as hand drums and guiros playing two phrases each of **A**, then two other groups of instruments, such as sleigh bells, shakers, playing the **B** phrases, and two other groups of instruments accompanying the **C** phrases. The children will enjoy following the plan on the board and coming in at the right moment with their instruments.
- Appraise the piece at the end, discussing whether or not everyone was properly on the beat or whether the percussion sometimes lagged behind. Also discuss whether or not the percussion instruments drowned out the music of the CD, or vice versa, and make adjustments to the numbers in the various groups or to the volume of playing, accordingly.
- If you want to extend this work at any point, you might like to have one group of instruments playing on the first of three beats and another group playing more lightly on the second and third beats.

Singing *Magic Carpet*

- If there is time sing the song through with track 9. Sing quietly and concentrate hard on keeping in time. Divide the class into two groups for the second part of the chorus where one part imitates the other.

Lesson 4

Objectives:
- To continue to develop **pitch** skills
- To work with **ostinati**
- To create a percussion accompaniment to the song *Magic Carpet*

Additional Resources:
- Copies of the *Steps* sheet for everyone
- Lyrics of the song *Magic Carpet*

Passing claps round the circle
- Here's a different version of the activity for a warm-up, which links in with the song *Magic Carpet*. The first person claps four crotchets, the second, three crotchets, the third, four crotchets and the fourth three. Continue like this.
- Don't fall into the trap of clapping like this:

This is what you *should* be clapping:

Steps
- *You* need a pitched percussion instrument placed so the children can't see it. Play any note then play a second note that is either one note (step) higher, one note (step) lower or exactly the same. Ask the children to simply state 'higher' 'lower' or 'same'. Play a third note. Was this higher, lower or the same as the second one? This is just to establish the way the following activity works.
- Now give out photocopies of the *Steps* sheet at the back and try a written version of the same thing. Ask the children to put a dot on each following vertical line to show the steps of the melody you play. If they join up the dots they can clearly see the shape of your melody. See the example below.

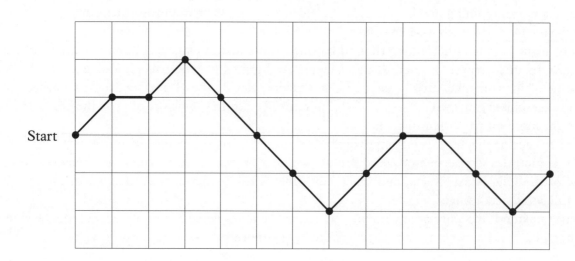

Inventing an accompaniment for the song _Magic carpet_

- As a class, make up a very simple percussion accompaniment using different ideas for the three different sections of the song: 1) chorus, part one, 2) chorus, part two, 3) verse. There might be only three or four children playing. Remember an accompaniment is there to _enhance_ the piece. If you find this is not happening, abandon it! It's all good appraisal work.
- Talk about whether there should be louder and quieter parts to this song. Do you want any lines to be sung solo?
- Now give a stunning performance of this song with the CD (track 9), and with the percussion accompaniment if you want. Everyone should stand like a choir and really let their voices sail.

Passing claps round the circle

31

Lesson 5

Objectives:
- To develop rhythmic skills
- To learn to 'layer up' **ostinati**
- To learn the new **sol-fa** note – **la**

Additional Resources:
- Copies of *Dustman's Drudge Accompaniment* sheet
- Copies of the *Rhythm Patterns 1* sheet
- Lyrics of the song *Magic Carpet*

Passing claps around the circle
- Repeat this activity from the last lesson, alternating crotchets in 3-time and 4-time

Rhythm-clapping practice in 3-time and 4-time
- First remind the children of the dotted minim note value they learnt in Lesson 1.

- Now write or project the two pieces below onto the board.

- Work out how to clap them both. Count yourselves in with *two* bars of three or one bar of four, respectively.

Dustman's Drudge with ostinati
- Give out photocopies of the *Dustman's Drudge Accompaniment* sheet.
- Divide the class into five groups and give out tambourines to group one, claves to group two, finger cymbals to group three and shakers to group four. Group five will be chanting the words of the poem so each line precisely fits into eight beats. (Later you can swap the groups around.)
- The numbers 1–8 written across the top of the sheet represent the eight **beats** of every line of the poem. So while group five are chanting the words of the poem, the other groups should follow their own line of instrumentation, playing their instruments on the exact beats as shown, and returning to the beginning of the line to repeat it, making six play-throughs in all, which is the duration of the poem. These repeated rhythms are called **ostinati**.

Dustman's Drudge with more complex ostinati
- Divide the class into two. Half the children are going to say the *Dustman's Drudge* poem while the other half repeatedly clap bar seven of the 4-time piece *(Rhythm-clapping practice)* above. The bar will fit into the poem twelve times.
- Now take a second rhythm from the 4-time piece – any random bar. Divide the class into three groups – one to say the words of the poem, one to gently clap the first rhythm and one to tap the second rhythm on the floor.

- Continue to 'layer up' **ostinati** in this way, but take care not to create such a thick texture that the various parts can't be heard very well. As well as clapping gently and tapping the ground, you might like to use tongue clicks, finger clicks and the mouth sound 'sh'.

Introducing a new *sol-fa* note – *la*

- Sing up the scale from **do** to **high do**, showing the hand signs for the notes you know.
- Now show the hand sign for **la** (**A** on the glockenspiel).
- Play track 5 of the CD. The children should echo the third set of eight sequences, which include the note **la**.
- You might like to try the following extension to this activity, but don't worry if it is beyond the capabilities of the children. Play the three-note sequences below but don't sing the **sol-fa** sounds as you play them, and see if the children can sing the right sounds back with the right hand signs. Sing the very first note, though. You will notice that the first note of each sequence is the same as the last note of the previous one, to make pitching easier. If the majority of the class are getting the pitch sounds right the activity works well. If you are getting many diverse responses there is no value to the work. However if you ask individual children to respond, this is a great pitch assessment activity.

1)	C	E	G		2)	G	E	D
	do	mi	so			so	mi	ré

3)	D	C	E		4)	E	G	A
	ré	do	mi			mi	so	la

5)	A	G	A		6)	A	G	C
	la	so	la			la	so	do

Working in 4-time with the new note *la*

- We are going to repeat the activity *Hear the rhythm, see the rhythm* again here, but now including the new note **la**.
- Give out copies of *Rhythm Patterns 1* and carry out the activity precisely as in Lesson 3 using the examples below, or inventing your own – but do keep it simple. You might have to play each example two or three times. Do as few or as many as time allows.

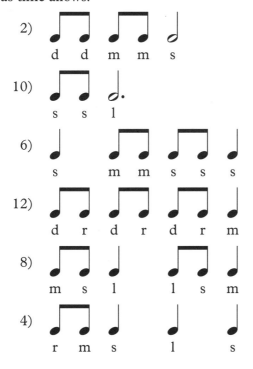

Singing *Magic Carpet*

- If there is time, finish with a performance of this song, with or without the accompaniment from the last lesson.

From here, go to Chapter 5 (page 56) for help with devising your own lesson plans from the various headings in Chapter 6 (page 63). Good luck!

Chapter 3
Year 5 – Five Lesson Plans

Overview of the five lessons – Medium-term plan

Theme: Pop

Music to listen to: *Baby Elephant Walk* by Henry Mancini

Concepts:
- Pop music
- Semiquavers
- The stave and pitched notes written down

Medium-term objectives:
- To introduce pop music – three big influences – Queen, Abba, The Beatles
- To learn to work effectively in groups
- To extend rhythmic understanding to include semiquavers
- To develop rhythmic and pitch skills
- To learn how pitched notes appear on a stave
- To be able to write pitched notes from aural dictation

Song: *Now is Now*

Resources:
- The course CD
- Lyrics for the song *Now is Now*

Additional Resources:
- Sticky coloured tape or coloured wool or lengths of string (See *Learning how the notes sit on the stave* – Lesson 2)
- CD of *Baby Elephant Walk* by Mancini
- Copies of the *Semiquaver Patterns* sheet
- CD with hits by Queen
- CD with hits by Abba
- CD with hits by The Beatles
- Copies of the *Blank Staves* sheet

Lesson 1

If the children are new to this scheme of work, so haven't worked through the set lesson plans for Years 3 and, 4, it is essential that you do that now, before embarking on the lessons that follow. It might take you less than a term to get through the ten lessons, but it is important that you and the children have a solid foundation of knowledge, understanding and skills before embarking on this more challenging Year 5 work.

If the children have worked from the scheme for at least a year, but you are not a musician and are new to the scheme, you will need to take time to study the set lessons for Years 3 and 4 to get a clear understanding of the work covered.

Objectives:
- To improve co-ordination with a new exercise
- To introduce **semiquavers**
- To develop pitch sense
- To listen to *Baby Elephant Walk* by Henry Mancini

Additional Resources:
- Copies of the *Semiquaver Patterns* sheet
- CD of *Baby Elephant Walk* by Henry Mancini

Crazy Creatures
- This is a great new introductory activity, but it's tricky, so we are learning it over three lessons!
- First, as a class, discuss which animals/birds can be shown simply by an action. See the list below and the photos. You will probably be able to think of others.

worm – wiggle finger
snake – wiggle both hands, palms together
crocodile – straight arms in front. Hands clap to show jaws
elephant – show trunk
koala – hands to rope (tree) climbing action
chicken – elbows do wings
deer – show antlers on head
butterfly – cross hands and flutter fingers
monkey – beat chest
giraffe – raise one arm straight up to show neck
kangaroo – show front paws

Koala

Chicken

Giraffe

Butterfly

- Divide the class into groups of seven or eight children. Each group should sit in a circle. Within each group each person should choose to be a certain creature. It doesn't matter if people choose the same creatures as people from another group, but within any one group, all the creatures must be different.
- Now, one circle at a time, go round the circle, each child saying the name of its creature while doing the action twice. Keep precisely to a beat throughout.

Introducing semiquavers

- Semiquavers can be written in pairs or fours. You will see from the illustration below that semiquavers have half the duration of quavers so semiquaver claps will sound twice as fast as quaver claps.
- Write this up on the board and clap down the 'triangle'. Make sure you choose a very slow tempo for the semibreve at the top – (saying 'one and two and three and four and' slowly helps) – so that you are able to fit all sixteen semiquavers in on the bottom line. The shorter the notes, the smaller the clapping action and the quieter the sound of the claps.

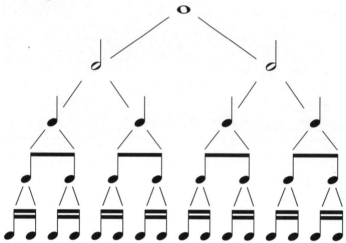

- Now, either give out photocopies of the *Semiquaver Patterns* sheet or write/project the patterns up on the board.
- Listen to the CD (track 23) and simply clap each rhythm straight after it has been played on the claves. Follow each pattern on the board or the sheet while it is being played on the CD and while you are clapping it back.
- With the class, invent some of your own patterns and clap them through.

Pitch work

- Start, as usual, by playing up the scale from **do** (C) to **high do** (C) on a pitched instrument while the children sing each sound and show the hand signs (**do, ré, mi, fa, so, la, ti, do**)
- Now play only the six notes the children have learnt so far and ask them to sing them and show the hand signs as you play each one – **do, ré, mi, so, la, do (high)**.
- Now play a pitched instrument to improvise sets of three notes for them to copy, first singing the **sol-fa** sound as you play each note, and then seeing if the children can manage to sing the right sound if you only *play* the sounds rather than singing them at the same time. See the examples below.

do, mi, so   **so, la, do (high)**   **ré, la, so**   **do, mi, ré**

- Extend this by playing the fourth set of eight **sol-fa** sequences, on the CD (track 5) for the children to copy.

Baby Elephant Walk by Henry Mancini

- Simply listen to this fabulous piece of music to finish. Remember that 'pop' is short for 'popular' and this piece is an extremely popular piece of classical music. The children will automatically move to the music and some will comfortably let themselves go. For the sake of more self-conscious children decide on say four actions such as toe tapping, knee tapping, finger clicking, shrugging one shoulder, and give the children the choice of sticking to those actions or moving freely.

Lesson 2

Don't worry about the apparent length of this lesson. Much of it is necessary explanation for non-specialists of how musical notes are written down on the lines and spaces of the stave.

Objectives:

- To start to understand how pitched notes are written down on the **stave**
- To find out about the big influences in pop music – Queen
- To start to learn a new song – *Now is Now*

Additional Resources:

- Sticky coloured tape or coloured wool or lengths of string (See *Learning how the notes sit on the stave*)
- CD with hits by Queen, including *Bohemian Rhapsody*
- Lyrics of the song *Now is Now*

Crazy Creatures

- Either choose new creatures or stick to the ones you had in the last lesson. Divide the class into circles of seven or eight children as before and go round each circle simply saying the name of your creature twice, while doing the action, as in the last lesson.
- Now, choose a circle as well as a child within that circle to set the whole thing going. That child should say the name of his or her creature twice while doing the actions, and follow it immediately with the name of another random creature in the circle, twice, while doing the action for *that* creature. The child whose creature was named must take over immediately, keeping strictly to the beat, by naming his or her own creature twice, while doing the actions, and then another random creature from the circle, twice. Keep going like this. You can name creatures that have already been named if you want, as long as no one in a circle is left without a go at all. When the circle goes wrong (by falling behind the beat), the next circle has its turn, and so on.
- See which circle manages to last the longest! Here is an example of what might be said:

1st child: 'elephant elephant deer deer'
2nd child: 'deer deer butterfly butterfly'
3rd child: 'butterfly butterfly deer deer' (back to…)
2nd child: 'deer deer chicken chicken'
4th child: 'chicken chicken worm worm'
etc.

Starting to understand how tunes are written out

1. What is a stave?

- It may be that your children have already learnt the concept of the musical stave if they learn an instrument such as the recorder, violin, piano etc. If all the children are familiar and confident enough with reading music from a stave, you can omit this part of the lesson. However, if the children have only a sketchy knowledge of how it all works, this is an ideal opportunity for improving note-reading skills.
- First show the children any of the songs included in this book. Point out the **staves**. This is the name for the five lines that are set very close together and go right across the page. (Because the songs in this book are written out with the piano part, and the piano has a wide range of high and low notes, for piano music there are always two staves operating in tandem. Many other instruments, including the voice, need only one stave.)

2. The musical notes ABCDEFG

- Explain that every musical instrument produces different sounds (notes) that are named by the letters **ABCDEFG**. These seven letters are repeated over and over. Show this on a pitched percussion instrument with two beaters. Play the lowest **C** at the same time as playing the next **C** up. The two **C**s 'match' perfectly but we say that one is an **octave** (eight notes) higher than the other. Demonstrate that with the **D**s and the **E**s and so on.

3. The Major Scale

- Tell the children you are going to play a major scale. Play from **C – C** slowly. Now play it again but this time ask the children to join in singing **do, ré, mi, fa, so, la, ti, do**. The children are used to singing this sequence of **sol-fa** notes, but now they are learning that this particular pattern of sounds, which in the western world we sing instinctively, is called a **major scale**.

- For your own information, see what happens if you try to play a **major scale** by playing the notes from **E – E** on the glockenspiel. You will hear that it doesn't sound right. That is to say that it doesn't produce the same familiar pattern of notes to which we can sing **do ré mi** etc. This is because for scales other than **C major scale** we need notes that would be black on the piano, called sharps and flats. This is a very big and complicated subject and there is no need to worry about it in this course. I just wanted to give you a bit of background to allow for greater understanding of the association between the notes **ABCDEFG** and the **sol-fa** notes.

4. Learning how the notes sit on the stave – first the lines

- You need to make a big stave on the floor. If you have a floor on which it is feasible to stick five long lines of sticky coloured tape, allowing for a Year 5 child's shoe size to fit in between each line, fantastic! Otherwise use different coloured wool, or, failing that, just use five lengths of string and put something at the end of each string of the colour that the string is representing. See the stave below for the colours. It doesn't matter how you achieve the spots on the bottom line!

Black
Red
Blue
Green
Yellow with spots

- These colours have been chosen to aid the process of learning the letters. Tell the children that the stave is like a ladder with very wide rungs. Line some of the children up at the bottom of the ladder with their toes touching the bottom line. The rest of the class should watch from the sides and then swap in later so everyone gets a go at standing on the stave.

- First of all simply tell the children to step on the first line. It is important that they understand right from the word go that when you say 'on the line' you mean actually step squarely on top of it, and not 'on' in the sense that they write letters 'on' a line. Their shoes on the line are representing the 'blob' rather than the 'stick' part of a musical note. Next all step on the second line, then the third, the fourth and the fifth.

- Go back to the start position underneath all the lines. Tell the children to step squarely on the first line. 'Can you spot **E**? It is spot-E (spotty!) Now step on the second line. '**G** for **Green**.' Step on the third line. '**B** for **Blue**.' Step on the fourth line. 'Re-**D**.' Step on the top line – '(**F**)ind your own way of remembering this!'

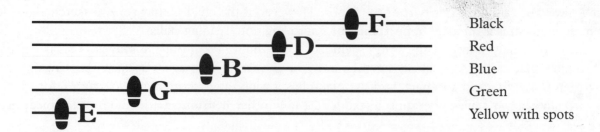

- Keep going over these notes by asking children to see how quickly they can find certain letters, and even making a team game out of it if you want.

- This kinaesthetic approach is most popular and effective, but there is always the simple mnemonic **E**very **G**ood **B**oy **D**eserves **F**ootball, to remember the notes on the lines (ascending) if you prefer.

Now for the spaces between the lines

- To learn the notes in the spaces, either use the mnemonic **FACE** or work the notes out from the lines.

	E
	C
	A
	F

- If the children take mini steps from line to space to line etc, and say the letters as they go, remembering that **G** leads back to **A**, they will be saying '**EFGABCDEF**'. You can now add the note that goes under all the lines – **D** (i.e. **D** comes before **E**) and the note on top of all the lines – **G** (i.e. **G** comes after **F**). Copy the stave below onto the board so the children can see a clear visual representation of the activity.

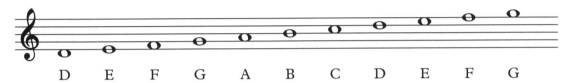

D E F G A B C D E F G

Pop Idols – Queen

- Queen was a heavy rock band, particularly popular in the 1980s, fronted by Freddie Mercury with his soulful yet driving voice and very individual appearance. The other three musicians in the group played guitar, bass and drums. Their song *Bohemian Rhapsody* is considered by some people to be the best song of all time.
- First divide the class into groups of five or six. Tell them that they are going to listen to the song *Bohemian Rhapsody* by the band Queen, and that you will then be giving the class a few moments for discussion in groups about their observations. The groups should nominate a spokesperson to give the rest of the class some feedback. Before you play the music give a few pointers about what kind of things they should be listening out for. The questions below should help prompt their discussion:
  - Did you like the music?
  - Why?
  - Did you notice how many sections it fell into?
  - Was there a story in the lyrics?
  - How is this music different from other pop music?
  - Was the singing always a solo or always more than one voice, or a mixture?
  - When there was more than one singer, did they all sing the same tune?

They might also be able to comment on the following elements of music with which they are now familiar: **dynamic(s)** (loud and quiet in music), **texture** (layers of sound in music), timbre (the quality of sound of different instruments, including the voice), **pitch** (is the music high or low or a mixture?) **tempo** (is the music upbeat, leisurely or other?).

- Now play short (approximately twenty to thirty seconds worth) extracts from other tracks on the CD. Simply ask the class to respond with a thumbs-up, down, or sideways to indicate whether they particularly liked the music. This might seem like a simplistic activity, but you are encouraging listening without too much stultifying analysis. The observations that will have emerged from the group discussions about *Bohemian Rhapsody* will give the children plenty of inspiration to allow them to make comparisons with the other songs on the CD, and to form opinions. Every so often ask an individual why they felt as they did about a particular track. If they are able to say something to strongly support their thumb signs, rather than 'Dunno, just did' – give plenty of credit!

Singing *Now is Now*

- Listen to the first verse of the song on the CD, track 24, while following the melody line on the musical score. Then play the track again and try to join in singing.

39

Lesson 3

Objectives:
- To find out about the big influences in pop music – Abba
- To work with **semiquavers**

Additional Resources:
- CD of hits by Abba
- Lyrics of the song *Now is Now*

Crazy Creatures

- First play the game as you did in the last lesson.
- Now try this new element. Set up a beat where everyone taps his or her legs twice then claps twice. All circles can practise this together briefly.
- Next we are going to incorporate the new element into the activity. While all circles keep going with the tapping and clapping as above, one chosen circle is going to incorporate the actions, as follows.
- When he/she is ready, the first child should break off from doing the tapping/clapping and change to doing the two actions for their creature (to fit in with everyone else's two taps) followed by the two actions for another random creature (to fit in with everyone else's two claps) That first child also says the name of his/her own creature and the name of the random creature while doing the actions, as before. The second child (whose creature has been named) then continues similarly, and so on. The extension is that, when you are not involved with saying the creatures' names and doing the actions, you must maintain the tapping/clapping, and move smoothly from one element to the other.
- As in the last lessons, when someone goes wrong or doesn't manage to keep up with the beat, swap to another group and so on. When you come back to the first group, start with the person who went wrong the last time.

Pop Idols – Abba

- We are going to work in a similar way to how we worked in the last lesson, when we listened to Queen.
- First explain that Abba is a group consisting of two men who were exceptional songwriters and two women with beautiful, distinctive voices. Abba's song arrangements were complex in order to be interesting, but the basic tunes were catchy and light enough for anyone to sing along to. The two women sometimes sang different tunes that blended together (in **harmony**), and sometimes sang the same tune (**unison**), but also took turns to sing **solo** parts.
- Divide the class into groups of five or six. The first task for the groups, when they have heard one of the Abba songs, is to try and come up with two contrasting words which explain the difference in style, in the most generic terms, of the music of Abba and of Queen, such as 'high and low' or 'fast and slow' or 'thick and thin'. If anyone says 'Dark and light' or 'Heavy and light', give them loads of praise!
- Can the children remember the various **elements** (pitch, timbre, texture, tempo, dynamics) on which they commented in the last lesson?
- Now play three more extracts of Abba songs, pausing in between to allow for group discussion. After each discussion one of the groups presents its feedback. You should hopefully get enough varying feedback to be able to listen all through to one last track together while considering all that was said in relation to the other tracks. Below are typical comments you might expect from the feedback sessions. If your particular class's feedback is less thorough than this, give more help along the way.
  – 'I liked the way the woman's voice started it all off with hardly any accompaniment and then it made a good effect when everyone started singing and playing'.
  – 'One of the women has got a higher voice than the other'.
  – 'It makes you feel like dancing because the beat never changes. It was quite a fast beat'.
  – 'There was only one place in the music when it went really loud, otherwise the dynamic stayed the same most of the time'.
  – 'I like the way they're all singing different notes which go well together.'

The last comment can be stated more musically like this: 'I liked the harmony that is Abba's trademark'.

Semiquavers in the words of a poem

- Take the poem below. It was originally used in Year 4 as a way of introducing graphic scores. In the version below a few words have been altered/added to accommodate this semiquaver work. Write the words of the poem, along with the given notation for the first line only, up on the board. As a class you are now going to try to work out the notation for the rest of the words. Do this a line at a time in the following way:
- First count the class in and all say the line very rhythmically together. Then ask an individual child to clap what was just spoken, then another child to say which beats are needed. Write the beats on the board above the words, even if the child is wrong, then ask for hands up for offers to correct what was given if necessary.

Dustman's Drudge

Mo - tor turn - ing, mo - tor turn - ing, jump-ing from the van and rush-ing to the bin, yeah!

Heave it high then trudge with the drud-ge-ry, fix it on the lor-ry and tip it all in, yeah!

Crash-ing, crunch-ing, grat-ing, munch-ing, churn-ing rub-bish in a splat-ter-to-nic spin, yeah!

Singing *Now is Now*

- Listen to the song on the CD (track 24). Then continue to learn the song with the help of the lyrics sheet.

Lesson 4

Objectives:

- To find out about the big influences in pop music – The Beatles
- To extend pitch skills
- To write down pitched notes from dictation
- To explore the structure of *Baby Elephant Walk*

Additional Resources:

- CD of hits of The Beatles
- Copies of the *Blank Staves* sheet – enough for everyone
- CD of *Baby Elephant Walk*
- Lyrics of the song *Now is Now*

Crazy Creatures

- Start with this activity.

Pop idols – The Beatles

- We could say that The Beatles 'invented' pop music, by moving away from the very predictable **Rock 'n' Roll** with its strong links to **Blues**. The Beatles' songs are very catchy, and in no way promoting any one member of the band with the others as a backing group. Their music combined with their whole style of hair and clothes turned them into enduring multimedia stars.
- Work in groups exactly as you did in the last lesson with Abba's music, and the lesson before with Queen's music, playing extracts of tracks from a Beatles album, and asking the groups to take turns to comment on their observations.

Pitch practice

- Write the three short pieces below up on the board exactly as they are written here with the rhythm and the start letter of the **sol-fa** sound. We have written in some of the notes on example 1 to get them started.

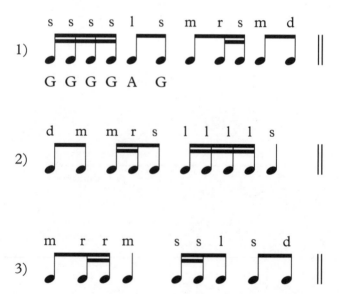

- If you play the first note of each piece on a pitched instrument (do = C) can the children manage to sing right through the pieces? Because some children have a better sense of pitch than others, the class won't necessarily all be singing the same sounds. If this is the case, choose individuals to have a go. If the child pitches a note wrongly play the correct note on the pitched instrument to steer them back.
- Finally check what you sung by playing the notes on a pitched instrument at the same time as the whole class sing through the pieces.

From sol-fa sounds to full notation

- Now give out copies of the *Blank Staves* sheet. See if the children can write out the three pieces on the board in full notation if **do** = **C**. We have written in some of the letter names on example 1 to get them started.

Listening to *Baby Elephant Walk*

- The children can either move freely or simply sit and listen. This time the point of the listening is to get a feeling of how many musical 'ideas' there are (three) and how each one can be described (see below):
  1. 'Introductory' bars
  2. Main tune
  3. Short rhythmic link to repetition of main tune
  4. Short, deep, loud notes followed by a fast jazzy passage on the saxophone
  5. As 4.
  6. The main tune 'exaggerated'

Singing *Now is Now*

- Finish by singing this song with the CD, track 24, or 25, which is the accompaniment.

Moving to Baby Elephant Walk

Lesson 5

Objectives:
- To consolidate work on the big influences in pop music – The Beatles, Abba, Queen
- To learn to write pitched notes from aural dictation
- To identify orchestral sounds in *Baby Elephant Walk*

Additional Resources:
- CD of hits of The Beatles, Abba, Queen
- Copies of the *Blank Staves* sheet
- CD of *Baby Elephant Walk*
- Lyrics of the song *Now is Now*

Crazy Creatures
- Start with this activity.

Pop Idols – The Beatles, Abba, Queen
- Divide the class into groups of five or six. Explain to the children that they are going to present to the class a 'review' of one of the three groups and their music. They can ask for extracts to be played on the CD player to support their points. It doesn't matter if more than one group wants to review the same band, but keep a good balance if possible.

Steps on a stave
- In Lesson 4 of Year 4, the children showed on squared paper the progression of a melody – stepping up, or down. Using aural skills in the same way, we are now going to show the melody on a **stave**. Write each note as a **semibreve**.
- Give out copies of the *Blank Staves* sheet and tell the children to write a semibreve note at the beginning of the stave on the G line. You are going to play twelve notes moving up and down by step (one letter name away) on a metallaphone, positioned so the children can't see it. Write down the twelve notes beforehand e.g.

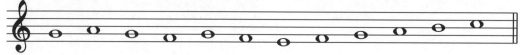

- Tell the children that they will get two goes at this exercise, so not to worry if they get lost while trying to write all the notes down. Start by playing G then slowly continue to play each note without stopping. The children should write down each note as you play it.

Listening to *Baby Elephant Walk*
- This time the point of the listening is to identify as many different instrumental sounds as possible. See below.
  Intro – violins and glockenspiel
  Main tune – muted* trumpet and piccolo, accompanied by piano, clarinets, drum kit and xylophone
  Main tune repeated – violins with interjections from tuba and bass drum
  Call and answer passage – trombones and woodwind or muted brass
  Solo – alto sax
  Call and answer repeated
  Solo – guitar
  Main tune – all instruments
  *a muted instrument produces a much less resonant sound. With brass instruments a pear-shaped stopper is pushed into the bell to produce this distinctive sound.

Singing *Now is Now*
- If there is time, finish with this song, with track 25 of the CD.

From here, go to Chapter 5 (page 56) for help with devising your own lesson plans from the various headings in Chapter 6 (page 63). Good luck!

Chapter 4
Year 6 – Five Lesson Plans

Overview of the five lessons – Medium-term plan

Theme: Celebration

Music to listen to: *Celebration Overture* by Philip Lane

Concepts:
- Jazz
- Blues
- Tied notes
- Syncopation
- Dotted crotchet and single quaver

Medium-term objectives:
- To learn about jazz music
- To learn about tied notes and syncopation
- To compose pieces including tied quavers
- To learn about the dotted crotchet and single quaver
- To listen and recognise instruments
- To read and play 'whole class' pieces, including non-pitched instrumental parts
- To write in full notation by ear
- To learn a song from the Caribbean

Song: *Sing an' Jump Up for Joy*

Resources:
- The course CD
- Lyrics of the song *Sing an' Jump Up for Joy*

Additional Resources:
- CD of any jazz music you like (optional)
- Copies of the *Blank Staves* sheet and pencils
- Copies of *Syncopated Shopping*
- Copies of *This Old Man*
- Copies of the *Twelve-bar blues* sheet

Lesson 1

If the children are new to this scheme of work, so haven't worked through the set lesson plans for Years 3, 4 and 5, it is essential that you do that now, before embarking on the lessons that follow. You might well get through the fifteen lessons much more quickly than in a term and a half, but it is important that you and the children have a solid foundation of knowledge, understanding and skills before embarking on this more challenging Year 6 work.

If the children have worked from the scheme for at least a year, but you are not a musician and are new to it, you will need to take time to study the set lessons for Years 3, 4, and 5 to get a clear understanding of the work covered.

Objectives:

- To develop rhythmic and co-ordination skills
- To introduce **Jazz**, including the words and sounds: **Blues**, **Boogie Woogie**
- To learn about the drum kit and to co-ordinate sounds and actions
- To identify the sounds of different instruments

Passing names and rhythms

- This warm-up activity develops quick thinking, co-ordination and rhythmic skills.
- Sit in a class circle. Any child can start, and each child is responsible for eight steady crotchet beats. During the first four beats, the child does two knee-pats, followed by two finger clicks while saying their own first name twice and then someone else's first name twice. The other four beats comprise a 4-time rhythm that the child invents on the spot and claps. The person named then continues without a break with the patting/clicking pattern and their own invented rhythm. Everyone else should continue with the knee-patting and finger-clicking to maintain the pulse. See the example below to get started:

1	2	3	4	5	6	7	8
Tom	Tom	Ellie	Ellie				
Ellie	Ellie	Stephanie	Stephanie				
Stephanie	Stephanie	Luke	Luke				

Introducing Jazz

- First explain that **Jazz** originated from Africa. It is helpful to show a world map and to explain about the passage of slaves.
- There are many styles of jazz. We'll look at two of them in this lesson.
- **Blues** is often played by small groups of musicians or solo guitar accompanied by mournful but gutsy vocals. John Lee Hooker is a great exponent of **Blues**. Listen to track 26 on the CD for a short original piece called *Twelve-bar blues*.
- **Boogie Woogie** is like a fast **Blues** played on solo piano with a heavy rolling bass. Listen to track 27 on the CD.

Getting in the groove

- Now listen to track 28 on the CD, which is a great jazz piece called *Getting in the Groove*.
- Listen again to the piece and join in clapping on the first beat of every four. When this is established, *you* start off a new beat by clapping on the first and the third beats of every four, and finally change to the second and the fourth.
- Play a short part of the track again with three people standing up to demonstrate how those claps can all work together.
- Number off the circle so everyone is 1, 2 or 3. Play a part of the track while the three different groups (1,2,3) clap the three different patterns simultaneously. One group might all clap above their heads and another

group turning slightly so they're clapping out of the circle, the third group clap normally.

- This time when you play the track, continue with the 'three group' clapping activity but instead of clapping, try finger clicks. When you point to a child, that child claps any rhythm or beat they'd like. Another signal indicates that the child should go back to clicking with the rest of the class. Continue like this, giving various children clapping solos.
- Choose a few people to play the established beats on non-pitched instruments. Don't have too many or you'll drown out the CD.
- Pass instruments one place to your left so others have a turn.

Rock Beats – sounds

- Listen to track 29 of the CD to hear the drum kit. Can the children pick out the sounds of the bass drum, the hi-hat, the tom and the snare?
- Divide the class into four groups to represent these four parts of the drum kit in a class piece. Copy the four parts below onto the board.
- Making the vocal sound given, each group repeats the given bar as many times as you want. Count the children in and see if they can achieve all four parts at the same time straight away without practising individual parts first.

	1	2	3	4
Bass drum:	*boom*	𝄾	*boom*	*boom*
Hi-hat:	*tss*	*tss tss*	*tss*	*tss tss*
Tom:	*doom*	*doom*	𝄾	*doom*
Snare:	*cha-ka*	*cha-ka*	*cha-ka*	*cha*

Rock Beats – co-ordinating actions

- This is a good co-ordination exercise for drummers. The hands and feet are going to do four different things. You need to be sitting down for this exercise, preferably in a chair though it does work sitting on the floor if you bend your knees and keep your heels on the ground. The right hand should tap the right knee and the left, the left knee.

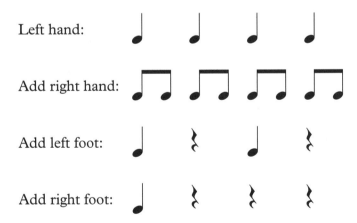

Lesson 2

Objectives:
- To learn more about **jazz** including the words and sounds
- To introduce **tied notes** and the word **syncopation**
- To start to learn a new song from the Caribbean – *Sing an' Jump Up for Joy*

Additional Resources:
- Piece of jazz music of your choice (optional)

Passing names and rhythms
- Start with this activity.

Getting in the groove
- Repeat some or all of the various activities from the *Getting in the groove* section of the last lesson. You might have your own CD with a suitable piece of jazz music to use for a change.
- Vary the beats from the last lesson by using clicks, claps, pats and vocal sounds.
- Try different beats and rhythms such as:

More Jazz
- First remind yourselves of the **Blues** piece (track 26) and the **Boogie Woogie** piece (track 27) from the last lesson.
- **Ragtime** is like a cross between classical and jazz music. It is strongly rhythmic. The children might have heard of Scott Joplin who is a famous composer of **Rags**, the most popular being *The Entertainer*. Listen to the **Rag** on the CD (track 30)
- **Dixieland Trad.** is another type of **Ragtime**, but is played by groups of instruments, such as bass, drums, sax, clarinet, trumpet, trombone. Listen to track 31.
- **Swing** is similar to **Trad.** but with drums and bass driving the music along rhythmically, while instruments such as clarinet and saxophone often play solos. Listen to track 32.
- **Bebop** sounds very much like Swing but messier! Listen to track 33.
- **Big Band** is **Swing** played by big bands! Listen to track 34.

Introducing tied notes
- As you will have heard in the Ragtime and Dixieland Trad. examples, Jazz music often contains **syncopation**. This means having a strong sound on a weak beat. We are going to start to learn about syncopation by learning about tied notes and all will become clear soon!
- Copy the piece below on to the board.

- Explain that the little curved lines joining two notes are called **ties** and that the second note is effectively 'tied' to the first note, extending the length of the first note by the value of the second. Try clapping this as a class, counting yourselves in. When you have clapped the fourth beat of the first bar keep the hands together and pulse them on the first beat of bar two. Continue like this, pulsing the first beats of the third and fourth bars too.

- Now copy up the piece below and try clapping it as a class when you have counted yourselves in.

- Divide the class into groups of four or five, and give each group like-sounding instruments. The groups take turns to play the piece twice through, each group following on without a break. The groups who are not playing could very lightly tap on beats 2 and 4 as an accompaniment. Can anyone improvise a tune to the given rhythm on the instrument they are learning, or on a recorder or metallaphone?

Learning a new song – *Sing an' Jump Up for Joy*
- Simply listen to this song on track 35 of the CD, noticing how much syncopation there is. This is a celebration song from Antigua with a typical **Rumba** rhythm. The **Rumba** is a Cuban dance.

Lesson 3

Objectives:

- To introduce **tied quavers**
- To compose pieces using **tied quavers**
- To continue to learn *Sing an' Jump Up for Joy*

Additional Resources:

- Copies of the *Blank Staves* sheet and pencils
- Lyrics of the song *Sing an' Jump Up for Joy*

Passing names and rhythms

- Start with this activity.

Introducing tied quavers

- When a note is tied to a quaver it works in exactly the same way as when it is tied to a crotchet, but you have to think a bit faster! Copy the bar in 4-time below, up on to the board but *without* the tie. Clap it through as a class, saying 'one and two and three and four and' as you clap.

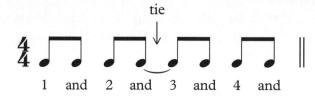

- Now write in the tie. Clap through the bar again, counting out loud, but don't clap when you say the word 'three', just pulse your hands to show that the previous beat has been lengthened.
- Work on the following rhythms in the same way. The last two have quavers tied to crotchets but work on exactly the same principle.

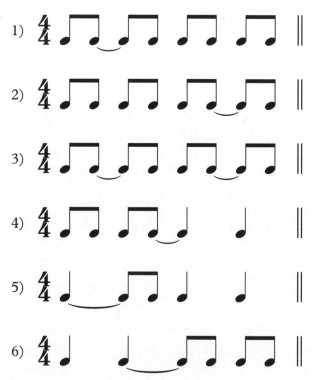

- Now arrange four of these seven bars (i.e. including the very first example) in any order to make a piece. Clap your piece through as a class. It might take a few shots to get it perfect.

Making up rhythmic compositions including tied quavers

- Divide the class into groups of five or six people and give out one *Blank Staves* sheet to each group. Allocate a scribe in each group. This child should write out any four of the seven bars above in a random order. (Because there are no pitched notes included, just write every note in the **F** space.) Next the groups should all practise clapping their respective rhythms. Walk round listening to the clapping and when a group can manage their piece successfully, they can help themselves to instruments (like-sounds within a group)

- As a class, listen to each group's performance. Work out which four rhythms each group used and in which order. Write these up on the board. Then play through all the different arrangements without a break.

Singing *Sing an' Jump Up for Joy*

- Play the CD (track 35) and, using the lyric sheet, try joining in with the lines 'This an' more have come to all our people' and 'Show the world that we are all one people'.

- Listen again and also join in with the words from 'Beaches plentiful' to the end of the song.

- Try singing through the whole song with track 35 to help you.

Lesson 4

Objectives:

- To extend work on tied quavers
- To extend knowledge of **intervals** and develop aural skills
- To listen to *Celebration Overture* by Philip Lane

Additional Resources:

- Lyrics of the song *Sing an' Jump Up for Joy*
- The piece *Syncopated Shopping*
- Copies of the *Blank Staves* sheet and pencils
- CD of *Celebration Overture* by Philip Lane

Year 6
Set Lessons

Singing *Sing an' Jump Up for Joy*

- Write up on the board the three rhythmic extracts from the song (below) without any words.

- Practise clapping each one as a class.
- Now write up the words and say the words as you clap the rhythms.
- Play the CD (track 35). Join in singing all the words except the bars you've been practising above, which you should clap.
- Finally try singing the whole song with track 35 and then with track 36, which is the accompaniment only.

Syncopated Shopping – working with tied quavers

- Either give out copies of this piece or project it onto the whiteboard.
- Try clapping through the first four bars as a class. Start by counting yourselves in with a slow pulse, bearing in mind that there are semiquavers to come. Work on accuracy if necessary then try clapping those same four bars while chanting the words at the same time. Work on the next two bars as a class, chanting the words and clapping at the same time, and allocate a soloist to play these two bars on a percussion instrument at the right time. Work on the last two bars of the piece then try it all through, including the soloist's bars.
- Choose other children to play the two-bar rhythms given as substitutes for the first solo, and then clap and chant and play through the whole piece!

Steps and skips

- In Lesson 5 of Year 5 (page 44), the children used their aural skills to follow a melody moving by step, and wrote down each note on the stave as you played it on a pitched instrument. Now we are going to try the same thing but including **skips** as well as steps, so that the melody might move *two* notes higher or lower. The proper musical term for a step is an **interval of a second**, and a skip is an **interval of a third**.
- Give out copies of the *Blank Staves* sheet and pencils, and play a G to start the melody. The children should write a semibreve G, and then write each following note by ear as you play it. Use the sequence of notes below:

Listening to a piece of music – *Celebration Overture*

- First discuss briefly which things we tend to celebrate in life. The children are likely to come out with the obvious birthdays, sporting wins, weddings, new babies, but try to think further – e.g. rain after a drought, safe return of a missing person etc. The *Celebration Overture* is not a piece that is constantly loud and strong and rhythmic, continually suggesting celebration. At times it is even thoughtful. If your class enjoys free movement, this is always a wonderful way to appreciate music.

- Listen to two or three minutes of the overture. The listening task for the children is to try and spot the sounds of the woodblock, the xylophone, and later the harp. Also notice how often you hear a tune repeated in a different way i.e. with different instrumentation or at a different pitch. This is called **imitation**.

Improvised movement

Lesson 5

Objectives:

- To extend knowledge of **intervals** and develop aural skills
- To write out a piece, from ear, in full notation
- To practise fitting new words to an existing piece of music
- To introduce a new rhythm – a **dotted crotchet** with a quaver

Additional Resources:

- Copies of the *This Old Man* sheet and pencils
- CD of *Celebration Overture* by Philip Lane
- The lyrics of the song *Sing an' Jump Up for Joy*

Year 6
Set Lessons

Steps, skips, flea jumps and frog jumps!

- In the last lesson we learnt that the musical term for a **step** is an **interval of a second**, and the musical term for a **skip** is an **interval of a third**. Now we are going to learn two more **intervals**: a **flea jump** or **fourth** and a **frog jump** or **fifth**.

- The children are going to work in pairs to try and write down in full notation, the song *This Old Man*. It is written below for your information. First give out photocopies of the *This Old Man* sheet. You will see that the starting note and bars 4 and 5 are given. So the children need to complete the piece by writing down what notes they think you are playing.

- Tell them that you will first play one bar at a time for them to write the *rhythm only* of the notes *above* the stave, initially. (It is easier to consider the rhythm first and then the pitch, rather than have to listen for both things at the same time). The rhythm for this song is very simple so you will only need to play each bar once.

- Next play the piece again, a bar at a time. Give the starting note – **G**, but tell the children to listen out for **steps** (**seconds**), **skips**, (**thirds**) and **flea jumps** (**fourths**) Tell them there is only one **fourth** and it is in bar 7. There is also just one **frog jump**, (**fifth**). Can they spot it in the given bar 5? You might have to play each bar more than once for the children to be able to get all the notes down. The results of this piece will give you a strong indication of the pupils' aural skills, general musicality and understanding of and knowledge of the notes on the stave.

- In a future lesson you might like to work from photocopies of a pupil's accurately written out version of *This Old Man* and perform the piece as a class using pitched percussion along with your own non-pitched percussion accompaniment.

This Old Man

Introducing the dotted crotchet

- Look at the rhythm below. It is the first of the two-bar substitute rhythms from the piece *Syncopated Shopping*, which we did in the last lesson.

- Now look at this second rhythm.

- It is the identical rhythm but written in a different way using a dotted crotchet instead of a crotchet tied to a quaver. The dot is therefore representing the tied quaver, which leaves a single quaver written with its own little tail. Try clapping the rhythm while following the new way of notating it.
- If the children understand this concept it will be their passport to many pieces of music. In *Mix and Match – Reading and writing music notation and graphic scores* (page 81), you will find an activity that will help reinforce this work.

Celebration Overture

- Stand in a class circle. Everyone should have a random percussion instrument. If you point to a child, (s)he should step forward, along with the two people on either side of him/her, and accompany the music for about ten to fifteen seconds playing whatever seems to suit the style of the music at that moment. The three people should naturally find a mutual style and beat/rhythm by being sensitive to each other.
- You might like to use this music as a springboard for some story writing at another time. Imagine that the whole piece is the story, building up to the celebration at the end. It's true that the greatest feel of celebration in the piece does indeed come at the end.

Singing *Sing an' Jump Up for Joy*

- First work on this accompaniment for maracas:

- The > signs are called **accents**. **Accents** tell you to play that note with a little extra force, making these three quavers louder than the other three.
- See how many shakers you need to create a good balance with all the singers. Add any other accompaniment you think will suit the song and give it some nice Caribbean colour. You might like to include 'homemade' instruments, such as pans with wooden spoons, or things around the room, like a metal waste paper bin. You could also include claps and even dance if you want.
- Go for a final performance of this song with track 36!

From here, go to Chapter 5 for help with devising your own lesson plans from the various headings in Chapter 6 (page 63). Good luck!

Chapter 5
How to plan your own lessons using the *Mix and Match* section of the book

This chapter deals with the principals of music teaching: how to structure a lesson by using activities or extensions of activities from any of the set lesson plans which will develop all the children musically, and be rewarding and fun. Don't skip this section, as it's vital!

The pointers below explain how to proceed. First it should be said that all of the activities in the *Mix and Match* section fit into more than one category. For example as well as developing pitch skills, when singing you are also working on rhythm and learning about composition, from the structure of the song.

Keep these principles at the front of your mind all the time:
- Let's turn the tide of insensitivity and encourage alertness and sensitivity
- Let's re-create a **respect for sound** and for our own sound parameters
- Let's be very critical about the sounds we create, particularly in performance, aiming for the highest possible standard of musical competence and creativity
- Let's make music education fun but keep our expectations high
- Let's inspire children
- Let's keep children active in mind or body or both whether they are listening, making music or composing
- Let's remember that the more positive the contribution, the greater the rewards

Keep these skills in mind:
- Listening
- Looking
- Thinking
- Communicating
- Focusing
- Memorising
- Co-ordinating
- Being 'in time'
- Being 'in tune'
- Being involved

Follow these general rules:
- Have aural, visual and kinaesthetic elements to every lesson.
- Have *at least* three different starting points in a lesson, taken from at least two different headings.
- Try to have a breadth and balance of activities within any one lesson and throughout the term.
- Don't be afraid to repeat activities as often as you want, either because it is a popular activity and therefore creates a bit of light relief after a more demanding activity, or because the children need more time with the activity to develop the required skills and/or to master the concept. You will notice how the learning in the set lessons is strongly spiral, where activities are taught and then revisited and extended.
- Don't be afraid to go off at a tangent if say, you are suddenly inspired by a piece of music you have heard.
- Start with a warm-up activity and keep the same one for quite a few lessons.
- Have instruments/cards/other resources at the ready.
- Have zero tolerance for 'twiddling' and for sound that interferes with the purposeful sound you are making.
- It doesn't matter if what you had planned for one lesson spills over into the next. If you achieve the equivalent of ten lessons of forty-five minutes per term, working in this way, you will be giving the children a very worthwhile and fun music education, and if you're achieving this as a non-specialist, you should feel proud

of yourself! But music is all about performance, so it is understandable that practising for say, an assembly or Harvest Festival, will take time from this music curriculum.

Devising the lesson – nitty-gritty
- Beside every activity in the *Mix and Match* section there are numbers indicating the youngest year group(s) for which the activity is suitable. For example, it's absolutely fine to use a Year 4 activity in Year 5.
- In the cases where you see that an activity is suitable for more than one year group, bear in mind that the level of work produced might be reflective of the age group in terms of one or more of the following: technical ability, imagination, communication skills, leadership skills, rhythmic/pitch skills.

Sorting out a medium-term plan – i.e. half a term's work
- Use the same headings as I have used. You might find that the objectives and concepts overlap considerably with mine because you are broadening, deepening and consolidating the skills and concepts learnt in the first five lessons of the academic year.
- Your choice of theme might be informed by the piece of classical music you intend to introduce, or by the song(s) and or rap, or it might be more abstract – e.g. Speed, Contrast or Focus. There's no real need to have a theme, except that it is a good way of linking a half term's work.
- Over the half term try to have a good spread of work from the six different areas of the *Mix and Match* section listed below. In Years 3 and 4 there will be much less *Reading and writing music notation* because this is introduced into the set lessons in Years 5 and 6. The *Rhythm work* comprises the longest part of the *Mix and Match* section because rhythm lies at the heart of everything – literally – it is the heartbeat of life.

Below are the headings you'll find in the *Mix and Match* chapter, with some *more specific* rules relating to each of them:

1. Listening activities
- Take the warm-up activity from either this section or the *Rhythmic Work* section. It is a good idea to keep the same warm-up activity for half a term. Children focus immediately if they know what the start of the lesson is going to be.

2. Rhythmic work (not involving writing)
- Never start a piece without either counting children in or having a definite opening of some sort, to give a sense of performance.
- When you are trying to hear more than one rhythmic idea simultaneously, always have *like* instruments in each group.
- Make sure there is appraisal at the end of an activity – so it's often good to have the class in two halves to discuss which half was the more accurate or the more expressive, depending on the activity. It is worth reiterating the 'no twiddling' rule here.
- In the *Mix and Match* section there are many activities for which you might like to use a backing track, simply to keep you perfectly in time. Track 2 of CD1 is invaluable for practice at hearing how four different pulses fit together and might provide useful support in certain activities.

3. Pitch work and songs
Tips for singing
- Always be relaxed and sitting up straight.
- It is best to use an OHP or whiteboard to present the lyrics so the children are not hunched over rustling papers.
- To warm up children's voices and to develop their pitch sense, repeat the sol-fa work from the set lessons.
- Look for ways of developing rhythmic skills or composition skills when working with a song. Don't always simply learn to sing it. Sometimes include solos, duets or ensembles.
- You will find pitch work and songs in the *Mix and Match* chapter, but as with *Teaching KS1 Music* I've deliberately not included many songs in this course because I wanted to use the time and space to help you with the difficult aspects of music teaching and to give you the most complete music course possible. So although it's fine to stick with just the songs in this book, please do feel free to sing any other songs you wish – there are plenty of good songbooks available.

4. Improvising and composing

First you need a stimulus:

Pictures

- The internet has many wonderful images that you can print off; encourage the children to 'think outside the box'. The picture might show a calm English country scene with hills, grass, trees, a stream, a few cows and a clear sky. Those listed elements might be represented on various instruments to create an atmosphere, but then you have to impose a bit of a story. Maybe a group of hikers appear and march across; maybe they break into a jog; maybe they pitch a tent ...

Poems

- A poem doesn't have to be riddled with 'sound' words or sound effects to be a good stimulus for composition. There might just be a sense of atmosphere or mood that is conveyed in various 'shades', which translates well into music. Once you start looking for poems, you will be spoilt for choice.

Stories

- The word 'story' is almost too grand. It is sufficient, for example, to take a picture as a stimulus and simply imagine what has just happened in the scene, or what is about to happen (see **Pictures** above).

Themes

- There is a list of themes in the *Mix and Match* section: *Improvising and composing* (page 80).

Getting started

- First, play any piece of music that you consider inspiring, in that it conveys a feeling or an atmosphere e.g. 'Mars, The Bringer of War' from *The Planets* by Holst. Ask the children to say what the music reminded them of and/or how the music made them feel. Tell them you are now going to reverse the process so that when *they* play their improvisation/composition, listeners would be able to say what the music conveyed to them.
- Either work on a single composition as a class, or work on separate compositions in groups.

Working as a class

- Sitting in a circle with loads of instruments in the middle is a great way to give a feeling of 'we're all working together', which is a very important consideration in group music making.
- Another approach is to set out a variety of instruments – pitched and non-pitched all over the floor. Put on a CD of something with a great beat – any style of music, to which the children will be inspired to walk in a funky way in and out of the instruments. When the music stops they should sit down in front of an instrument. If two people are arguing over an instrument, put a rhythm on the board and the child who claps it accurately gets to have the instrument.
- Of course everyone wants to feature the most highly in the piece, but there must be an understanding that within any piece some instruments will contribute much less than others because of the nature of the music you are making, but the children's playing time should come out roughly the same over the year.

Working in groups

- Sometimes it is good to let the children go off and work in groups, if there are available free spaces in school or on the playground. In this case, don't worry about setting down too many ground rules the first time. Call them back after ten minutes at the most, and insist on stringent performance conditions – i.e. silence before the start of each piece and appraisal at the end of each piece.
- The children's choice of instruments for their group can be commented upon in the appraisal part of the activity, and will inevitably be limited by availability of instruments. Occasionally it is interesting, if possible, to have the same combination of instruments in every group in order subsequently to compare and contrast the various group improvisations.
- During this appraisal time, individuals should offer constructive criticism – first of a positive nature and then 'ways in which the piece could be improved'. This kind of post-performance discussion will be more valuable than dishing out too many rules beforehand when the children will be desperate to play. There is nearly always one group who has prepared a stunning piece of work which will set the level for the next time the children work together, and throw up all sorts of ideas for them to apply to their work the next time. Below are some factors that determine whether a piece is stunningly effective:

1. Choosing instruments that work well together.
2. Playing them in varying ways.
3. Good communication within the group so everyone knows when they should be playing; maybe having a leader to subtly nod to indicate sounds starting or stopping, and times when the music should increase or decrease in volume.
4. Creating a piece that suitably conveys the given theme or stimulus and thus prompts the relevant emotion from the listeners.
5. Having a good length of piece – long enough but not too long – approximately thirty to ninety seconds.
6. Sometimes incorporating the spoken word or vocal/body sounds if appropriate.
7. Most importantly, you can always tell when a group has prepared well, getting straight on to task and brain-storming to get the best possible results rather than just messing around, because if asked to repeat their piece it would come out roughly the same the second time.

It is helpful to think of improvisations and compositions as falling into two categories:
1. Rhythmic
- Start with a beat or a rhythm and make sure all players are aware of the beat and keep to it throughout the piece.
2. Free
- The instruments are representing sounds/ideas, so might be 'scratched' or 'stirred' or 'shimmered' or generally played without the constraint of a beat.
- It might be effective, of course, to mix these two types within a piece.

5. Reading and writing music notation and graphic scores
- Keep paper and worksheets (as needed) and pencils and clip boards at hand if you're in a hall or music room away from your regular classroom. Have a folder for each child. By the end of the academic year the folders should have quite a few sheets in them.
- Photocopiable sheets for activities can be found at the back of the book or on the ECD to be printed out as required.

6. Listening to music from other times and cultures
1. Classical (3, 4, 5, 6)
- The pieces of classical music on the list in the *Mix and Match – Listening to music from other cultures,* can be used for any year group in KS2. The different ways of getting the most out of the music, given below, might also be used right across the key stage, but *you* will know best whether or not your class will be comfortable with movement ideas. There is, however, *something* for everyone here.
- All the pieces listed are easily obtainable from music/CD shops or online stores. There are some very good value compilations of classical music to be found these days and the shorter pieces will almost certainly appear on a compilation CD.

Why listen anyway?
- I think it's important to be sure why we are listening to classical music in the first place (apart from it being a National Curriculum requirement!). It is great if even just one or two children from a class have a liking for classical music and are encouraged to listen to more. Classical music is quite a different experience to pop music. It rolls around your senses and evokes a whole range of pictures and emotions, not usually tapped by pop music. It's part of our history and often involves many musicians playing at the same time. So the volume is achieved not with a volume knob but with a swell of combined human effort, and because the **dynamic** (volume) is not constantly loud, the impact is greater. There's something magical about classical music.
- Listening to classical music doesn't have to be confined to listening to a recording. Listening to someone playing in a live situation can be very valuable.
- It is also extremely valuable to listen to classical music outside of the music lesson to encourage the idea that music is to be enjoyed rather than simply studied.

How to listen
- Choose the piece carefully. Make sure the music is only a few minutes long. Apart from those pieces with 'built-in' stories (more of that below), all the pieces on the list in the *Mix and Match* section are shorter than

four minutes. They have been chosen for their duration and because they are relatively easy to listen to.

- When we are familiar with music it heightens our enjoyment. But children find it difficult to simply sit and listen in silence to classical music so we need ways to make it stimulating rather than tedious. Read on …

Clapping to the music

- Either do this spontaneously, clapping at the most obvious pulse then randomly changing to a different one and returning to the first one, or pass claps around the circle, taking care to precisely match the beat of the piece of music. This was first taught in Lesson 1, Year 3; but also apply other variations of claps as taught subsequently. However, do take care that the clapping does not drown out the music.

Playing percussion instruments with classical music

- Children love this activity and are improving their listening skills while learning about **phrasing** (musical sentences), **beat**, playing in an **ensemble** (group), anticipating one's turn, style, mood, **dynamics** (louds and quiets) **timbre** (different sounds), **texture** (a greater or lesser number of instruments playing at once) and **structure** (the shape of the piece). They are also getting a strong feel for the balance of sound by not playing too loudly or quietly compared to the rest of the class and to the CD.
- Not all music lends itself well to having a percussion accompaniment. Make sure the piece is no longer than three minutes in duration, but preferably much shorter. Also check that the phrases are clearly defined so it will be possible for the different groups of children to recognise the moment in the music when they should start playing. If you can count repeatedly to eight, at a steady beat, throughout a piece of music, it is likely to be suitable for percussion accompaniment.

Stories with classical music

- There is, of course, nothing better than a story to bring music alive. The old favourites: *The Sorcerer's Apprentice* by Paul Dukas, *The Carnival of the Animals* by Camille Saint-Saëns, *Peter and the Wolf* by Sergei Prokofiev etc. are perfect for younger children.
- With older children, try playing any piece from the list and see what mood it evokes, then decide on a scene – a fairground, a jungle, a cave, a mountain, the sky, a planet, a forest, a factory, a shopping mall etc. Now work on the simplest form of a story, an example of an extract of which might be: 'This is where the robots step out from behind the tree and walk into the light of the enormous torch' *or* 'This is where the foam on the tops of the waves forms shapes that turn into people then dissolve into the sea' *or* 'This is where the carpet lifts off the ground, and goes through the roof, and this is where the wind catches it and whips it up, and this is where the people fall off it, and this is where all the parachutes open up!' It's great fun! You can do it off the cuff if you've got that kind of imagination or you can listen in advance and prepare some ideas.
- The next stage is of course for the *children* to think of what's happening. The important thing is to make sure your story is not drowning out too much of the music. It will inevitably impose itself a bit, but don't have story going on all the time otherwise the music becomes of secondary importance. Make sure that, having spent some time discussing images and events that might be happening, you then play the music again and tell the children to close their eyes and keep those images inside their heads.
- *Introducing Classical Music Through Stories,* published by Faber Music, consists of full colour illustrated stories specially written to 'match' the music. There are six books in the series, each packaged with a CD of the relevant piece of classical music. The pieces are between eight and thirteen minutes in duration, and are guaranteed to capture children's imaginations!

Creating pictures

- Music can often inspire great artwork. Pick up on the ideas you have already discussed and next time you listen to the music, ask everyone to imagine one particular scene, which they will then depict on paper. (It doesn't matter if several people want to use the same image.) Some examples follow.

Dylan, aged 7   Kieran, aged 7

How differently we respond to the same piece of music!

Drama with music
- Some children respond well to creating a short play to a piece of music. Again, let's take 'Mars' from *The Planets* by Holst. Listen for a minute or so to get the feel/style/atmosphere of the music, then work on a piece of class drama or work in groups to create short plays. The role of the music might be to create a background to dialogue and mime/action, *or* it might be played between action/speech.
- Alternatively your class might be inspired to work out an advertisement that would work well with a certain piece of music.

Moving with music
- This needs to be treated with care. If children have been used to moving to music throughout their music education they won't feel self-conscious and will really enjoy the experience. Otherwise, it might be better to leave this one out!
- We move to music in order to really 'feel' and better 'absorb' the music rather than just listening to it. In the set lessons for Years 3, 4 and 5 there was analysis and movement work connected with fast and fairly fast pieces of music with a strong beat. In the *Mix and Match* section there is an idea for movement to go with a slow piece of music, as well as other general movement ideas (pages 83–84).

Drawing/colouring while listening
- The children might be involved with decorating their folders or creating a poster to show the **elements** of music, along with their meanings (these words appear in bold print and can be found in the glossary, page 154). Whatever they are doing they should work in silence so they can enjoy listening to a piece of classical music at the same time.

2. Pop (5 and 6)
- There is no point in trying to teach Rap or Hip Hop to Years 5 and 6! They'll probably know more about it than you, so leave that one for out of school. They'll also be familiar with current pop music, but maybe less familiar with past pop influences, which is why three big influences feature in the set lessons in Year 5 – Queen, Abba and The Beatles. Don't overdo this aspect of music, but simply listen to a few more songs from each of these three influences, and/or others that you like, over the course of Years 5 and 6. Work in the same way in which you did in the Year 5 set lessons.
- Some of the ways of listening to classical music can also apply to pop, depending on the particular piece of music concerned, such as accompanying with percussion instruments, moving to the music and devising an advertisement that would work well with a particular song.

3. Jazz (6)
- Again, don't overdo this section, but simply introduce the children to a few more pieces of jazz during the academic year, working in the same way as for the set lessons in Year 6.

- In the *Mix and Match* section there is a list of jazz artists/composers to look out for when choosing recordings.

4. World (3, 4, 5, 6)

- It is good for children to experience as wide a variety of music as possible so this course wouldn't be complete without suggestions of music to listen to from other areas of the world. Don't worry if you don't have any knowledge of music from other parts of the world; just occasionally provide the opportunity for children to listen to such music as Chinese, Caribbean, African, South American etc. Now you have ways of listening to music at your disposal, the children will be equipped with the best possible chance of absorbing and enjoying it.

- You are likely to find a good selection of cheap compilations of world music in your local music shop or online retailer.

On your own

Moving to a jazz piece

Chapter 6
Mix and Match

Beside each activity in this section are numbers to indicate the youngest year group(s) for which the activity is suitable.

1. Listening activities – not involving rhythm
(Take warm-ups from this or the following section)

Signals (3)

- This was first introduced in the KS1 book. You need to devise up to a dozen different musical signals on percussion instruments, along with an associated action for all of them. See the examples below:

    C then the G above it on a pitched percussion instrument = stand up
    Reverse those two notes = sit down
    C followed by a higher C = hands on heads
    E followed by the C below it = kneel
    Three clave taps = clap three times
    Shaker = fold your arms
    Two drum taps = hands on hips
    Two woodblock taps = hands on shoulders
    etc.

- Play a random signal. The children have to think quickly and respond with the correct action. Whoever is late or wrong is out. Keep eliminating children until you have a winner.

Animal Ark and other pairs (3, 4)

- This was introduced in Year 4, Lesson 1, and is a great way to develop 'scan' listening. Vary the game by using words rather than sounds. You might choose pairs of countries, colours, boys' or girls' names or any other theme of your choice.

Find Rumplestiltskin (3)

- This game was introduced in KS1 and is another activity that develops 'scan' listening. One person (the finder) hides their eyes while you silently nominate one of the class to be Rumplestiltskin. At the signal to start everyone repeatedly says his or her own name at a medium volume except for the nominated person who repeatedly says 'Rumplestlitskin'. How quickly can the finder discover Rumplestiltskin?

Identifying voices (3, 4)

- Members of the class would probably have no difficulty recognising the voices of other members of the class. But would they be able to identify a *singing* voice? Unlikely. Format the game in any way you want – a circle with a blindfolded person in the middle or simply have someone with his or her back to the rest of the class. The singer could sing **so mi do**, or something of your choice. If pupils are reluctant to sing they could say someone's name in a different voice tone with a different accent.

Identifying recorded instruments (4, 5, 6)

- Listen to tracks 10–22 of the CD and try to identify the sounds of the instruments of the orchestra.
- Listen to any piece of classical, world, pop or jazz music and try to identify the instruments.

Identifying live instruments (3, 4, 5, 6)

- Divide the class into groups of five. Each group needs a leader who has a pencil and paper to hand. While one group takes five or six instruments behind a screen or somewhere out of sight, the other groups hide their eyes.

The group behind the screen silently nominates a singer/speaker. The leader counts to four and the group then play their instruments rhythmically in a short improvised piece which lasts for about ten seconds and includes a few brief vocal sounds by the nominated member. The other groups then confer and each leader writes down which instruments they thought they heard and whose voice it was. You take the papers in and allocate points for correct instruments named.

- Continue until all the groups have had a turn at playing, then count up the points to see which group has won.
- To increase the difficulty of this activity, make the improvisation even shorter.

2. Rhythmic work – not involving writing
(Take warm-ups from this or the preceding section)

Clapping two different beats at once (teacher and class) (3)
- You clap to a **crotchet** beat while the children clap at the same time to a **minim** beat. When everyone is comfortable with the two beats going on at the same time, always checking that the pulse remains steady and doesn't speed up, you say 'Swap!' and without a break the swap should happen.
- Try exactly the same exercise but with **crotchets** and **quavers** or with **crotchets** and **semibreves**.

Playing two different beats at once (teacher and class) (3)
- Try the above exercise with instruments. Divide the class into groups of five or six children. You have a drum and each group has like-instruments but of a different **timbre** from the other groups. You work with one group at a time, varying the combination of beats for each group you work with. Groups not playing should be listening ready to give feedback on the accuracy of the beats. Finger chimes and Indian bells work well for the semibreves because you can hear the sound ringing on for the full four crotchet beats.

Clapping two different beats at once (class in two halves) (3, 4, 5)
- The class should sit in two groups. Allocate a leader for each group. *You* play a steady beat on the drum throughout and take care not to speed up. The leader for each group can choose to clap quavers, crotchets, minims or semibreves and members of both groups join in with the beat set by their respective leaders. Once a beat is well established the leaders can swap to a different beat. It is unlikely that they will make the change at the same moment but it doesn't matter if they do. Neither does it matter if both groups happen to find themselves clapping the same beat at the same time.

Playing two different beats at once (class in two halves (3, 4, 5)
- Exactly as for clapping (above), but each group have instruments of a different timbre to create an effective contrast of sound.

Clapping/playing four different beats at once (4, 5, 6)
- As above, but with four leaders and four groups.

Clapping/playing different rhythms at the same time (4, 5, 6)
- As above but with rhythms. These activities work at many levels from simple to challenging.
- Take 4-time rhythms from *Rhythm Patterns 1* or the *Rhythm Patterns 3* (Year 6 only) sheet. Alternatively, invent some of your own.
- Either set out rhythms using the notation cards for the leaders to follow, or write the rhythms on the board. You might decide on four different rhythms and ask the leaders to choose one each to start with.
- Extend this activity by having three rhythms instead of two but listen carefully to the three rhythms working together to check there is a good balance of sound and that the texture is not too dense. Adjust the number of players in a group to correct the balance if necessary, and ask the children to play more quietly so they can really examine their own sound contribution.

Passing claps round the circle
All the following activities can be carried out at slow, medium or fast speeds. The speed determines the difficulty of the activity and hence the suitability of age group for each. It's great to take a piece of pop music with a strong beat as a backing track for the claps. (Choose a faster track for older children.)

1. Crotchets (3)
- The children should sit in a circle and 'pass' a clapped beat around. Firstly each child should clap four crotchets, then without a break continue round the circle a second time but only clapping two each, then the third time just clap one each.

2. Alternate different beats (3, 4)
- Always make sure that each child claps the equivalent of four crotchet counts. There are some examples below. The latter ones rotate three of the four different beats so require good memory and concentration.

3. Clap improvised rhythms in 4-time (3, 4, 5, 6)
- Children have to invent their own rhythm on their turn, but it *must* fit into a 4-time metre. Try out some examples with the children first, then work from the list of examples below or take examples from the *Rhythm Patterns 1* sheet or the *Rhythm Patterns 3* sheet (Years 5 and 6). Or invent your own rhythms.

Mix and Match

Body and mouth sounds to show four different patterns of crotchets and crotchet rests (3)

- Write the following four-time rhythmic patterns on the board:

- Divide the class into four groups and have a definite place for each group to sit which is then associated with a particular rhythm.
- First practise clapping through the four rhythmic patterns as a class, four times for each one.
- Now allocate one rhythmic pattern to each group and ask them to decide on a simple mouth or body sound e.g. ssh, oink, clicking fingers, clicking tongues, tapping hand sharply with two fingers, tapping knees, tapping the floor. Try two groups at a time and then all four. You keep everyone in time by playing e.g. a pair of claves gently, so the noises made by the children mustn't be too loud to hear your claves.
- Extend this by swapping the groups within a rhythmic framework in the following way: You suddenly swap the beat from the claves to the drum, for example. This is the signal for the children to have a whispered group conference to choose a new sound then to wait for you to change back to playing claves, which, following your count of four, sets off the four rhythms with the new sounds.

Four different groups of instruments play the four patterns at the same time (3, 4, 5)

- Making sure you have 'like' sounds within your group, try the above rhythmic patterns with four lots of different sounding instruments. Change the combination of crotchets and rests if you want.

Stepping and stopping (3, 4)

- This activity first appeared towards the end of Year 2, and will have presented a challenge to many children. It is well worth repeating the activity here to develop skills of internalisation.
- The exercise requires everyone to count up to eight repeatedly; play a quiet beat on the drum to help keep everyone in time. Play every single one of the first eight beats, then play only seven, and have a crotchet rest on the eighth, then only play six and have two rests for beats seven and eight. Continue like this, reducing the number of beats and increasing the number of rests until every one of the eight beats is a rest. (See the diagram)
- The children should take a step on your beats and stand still on the rests, so they need to keep counting carefully as they go on.
- After the eight silent, still beats, start to build back up to eight played beats (eight steps) as shown in the following diagram.

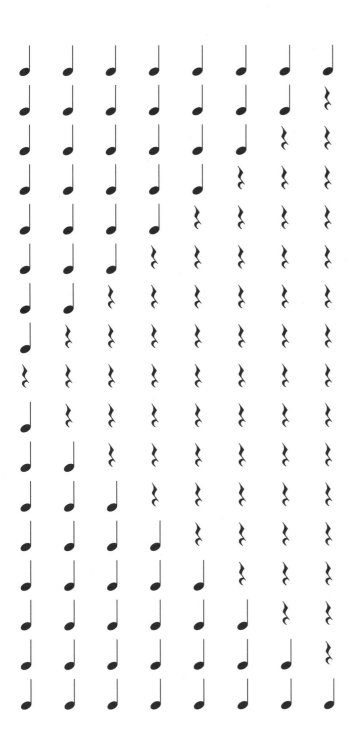

Visual representation of a one-bar rhythm (team game) (3, 4, 5)

- Divide the class into teams of four (you might have to swap children in and out according to the numbers in your class). The four children in the teams stand side by side and number off 1 to 4.
- Tell the children that they are each representing a beat of the bar. They must listen to what you clap and arrange themselves to 'look' like the rhythm they have just heard. Clap it just once initially, and then after a few seconds repeat it, and again if necessary. If they think you clapped a crotchet on 'their' number, they should stand still and straight. If they think you clapped a pair of quavers on their number, they should put their hands on their heads (representing the bar at the top of the pair of quavers) and if you show palms up, indicating a crotchet rest, on their number, they should sit down as though having a rest. The first team to arrange themselves in the right patterns to show a visual representation of what you clapped, gets a point. The first team to get three points wins. See the following examples:

$\frac{4}{4}$ ♩ ♫ ♫ ♫

$\frac{4}{4}$ 𝄽 ♫ ♫ ♫

Mix and Match

Visual representation of a two-bar rhythm (team game) (5, 6)

- Play the game as above, but have eight children in a team and leave a little gap between the children numbered 4 and 5 to show that the eight children are representing two bars in 4-time.
- If you want you can now include minims (two children standing shoulders touching), dotted minims (three children with shoulders touching) and semibreves (four children with shoulders touching i.e. the first four or the last four). For these longer notes keep your hands together after the clap and pulse them once for a minim, twice for a dotted minim and three times for a semibreve, to show that the sound is sustained. For rests, on the other hand, make a very deliberate palms-up gesture. If you have two consecutive rests, do the gesture twice. If you want to include semiquavers, the associated action should be hands and forearms overlapping on heads, to represent the double bar at the top of the semiquavers. The next photo shows children visually representing the following bar, which includes semiquavers:

Find the right notes (3, 4, 5, 6)

- Divide the class into teams of five or six. Number off the team members. This is to dictate the order of children to go and collect notation cards from a central spot.
- You clap any 4-time one-bar rhythm. The groups have a discussion about which notes are required for the rhythm you clapped. They should fold their arms to show they have done this. When a group is ready, send the relevant representative to collect the notes and bring them back. That person then lays out the cards on the floor to show the rhythm you clapped. When all the groups have done this, award points to correct 'answers'.
- Making harder rhythms including semiquavers increases the difficulty of the activity, as does clapping a two-bar rhythm.

Passing names across the circle (3, 4)

- Sitting in a circle, set up a beat where everyone taps the floor twice then clicks their fingers twice. The person who starts the activity says their own name twice as they tap the floor, then the name of someone else twice as they click. The named person then does the same and so on. Remember, the faster the speed of the set beat, the harder the exercise, but take great care to stick carefully to the beat throughout. Generally, boys find the co-ordination of the taps and claps/clicks more difficult than girls do.

Passing names of instruments across the circle (4, 5 and 6)

- This is the same as the activity above but instead of the children saying their own names they say the name of an orchestral instrument. So before starting the activity, allocate names of instruments to each child. The list below includes string instruments, then wind, brass and lastly percussion. Children representing instruments from the same family of the orchestra should sit together. Leave a little gap between families. Each child must remember what instrument they are, and use that name instead of their own name. The rule is that having said your own instrument's name twice, you should then say the name of an instrument from another family of the orchestra. You might prefer to split the class in two and use fewer instruments than those listed, according to your numbers.

Violin, viola, cello, double bass, harp
Piccolo, flute, oboe, clarinet, bassoon
Trumpet, trombone, French horn, tuba
Bass drum, kettle drum, snare drum

Recognise the rhythm elimination game (4, 5, 6)
- First write the numbers 1–10 on ten pieces of paper and put them round the edges of the room where they are visible to the children. You write ten different rhythms in 4-time on the board and number them. Clap one of them. The children must work out which one you clapped, note the number, and go to the place in the room denoted by that number. All those in the wrong place are 'out'. Bring the children who were correct back to the board for another rhythm and continue like this until you have a winner.
- Challenge the children with longer rhythms if they find it too easy. Include semiquavers at your discretion in the rhythms for Years 5 and 6. See the *Rhythm Patterns 3* sheet for ideas.

Password (3, 4, 5, 6)
- Write four different rhythms on the board and number them 1 to 4. The children each need a piece of paper for this activity. You are going to clap all the four rhythms in a different order. Clap each one twice and leave a gap between to give the children a chance to write down the order in which they thought you clapped the rhythms. So they will simply write 3 2 4 1, for example.
- Before you start clapping write your number order down on a piece of paper. At the end all the children must hold up their sheets and you ask the children who got the right combination to stand up. If there is no one, repeat with a different rhythm order, until there is! If there is more than one person, those people get to do the activity again, with a different order of rhythms.
- As an extension for Years 5 and 6, if there is still more than one person with the correct combination, clap the four rhythms in your pre-decided order without a gap.
- When you have just one child with a matching four-digit number, they have the 'password' and can choose the next activity in the lesson (or the first activity of the following lesson if you prefer).
- Another possibility is for the child with the 'password' to then do the teacher's job in the next game.

Internalisation activities
1. Mixing two metres (3, 4)
- See the activity *Mixing Metres* in Lesson 4 of Year 3 (page 19). Extend that by choosing a faster speed and/or by playing instruments instead of clapping.

2. Mixing three metres (4, 5)
- Add 2-time to the activity above.

3. Mixing unfamiliar metres (5, 6)
- Take any two numbers up to seven and try the same exercise as above, always stressing the first beat. Extend by trying three at a time. It is interesting to hear the pattern emerging, particularly if you have different sounds for the different metres.

4. Making beat patterns (4, 5, 6)
- Ask the children to each think of a number between 1 and 8. You tap crotchet beats on a woodblock, **accenting** the first of each group of eight. The children should say their number out loud on precisely the right tap, sticking to the same number throughout the activity. Some will have thought of the same number so there might be a loud vocal accent on some taps, no accent on others and a less pronounced accent on others. Continue for as long as you want. Just going through one set of eight beats would make for a very irregular sounding lot of beats, but going through several times will allow a pattern to emerge.
- Try the activity with different vocal sounds or try instrumental sounds.
- To extend, set a faster pulse.

5. Making beat patterns from a poem (4, 5)

- In the three short poems below there is a mixture of metres. The syllables to be stressed are underlined. You can hear the poems on the CD (track 37).

Pop

<u>Pop</u> goes the <u>pip</u> in the <u>grape</u>
And <u>pop</u> goes the <u>stone</u> from the <u>cherry</u>
And <u>pop</u> goes the <u>pea</u> from the <u>pod</u>
And <u>pop</u> goes the <u>cork</u> from the <u>bottle</u>
<u>Pop</u>!

Dreams

<u>Dreams</u> are <u>funny</u> things.
They <u>catch</u> us una<u>wares</u>,
Are full of <u>dares</u>,
And <u>no</u> dream is
What it <u>seems</u>.

The Circus Dream

I <u>went</u> to look at some <u>dreams</u> today,
They were <u>lined</u> up on a <u>shelf</u>.
I <u>liked</u> the look of the <u>one</u> about the circus,
And <u>took</u> that home for my<u>self</u>.

- Practise saying one of the poems as a class, clapping on the accented sounds.
- Now try saying it in your head while clapping at the right time i.e. internalising the words. Be critical of your attempts. The idea is that the whole class should be clapping at exactly the same moment. This will only happen if the children are saying the poems in their heads at exactly the same speed. Say it once out loud to get into the swing of the beat then try.
- Try the same thing but with instruments. Divide the class into groups of not more than eight and listen critically to each other's performances.

Speaking in canon (a round) (3, 4)

- First look at the sentence below that we have written out to show how each line fits into four beats. Listen to the CD (track 38) then divide the class into four groups and try saying it in canon exactly as you hear it on the CD.

1	2	3	4
When	I	came	to
school	this	mor	ning
all	of the	children	were
playing	out	-	side.

- Below are two more, written out as ordinary sentences. Can the class work out how to fit each sentence into four lots of four beats by speaking the words with a strong rhythm, a definite beat and with definite accents? N.B. The first accented sound of the first example is the first syllable of the word 'nothing'. Remember, sometimes there might be more than one syllable per beat. If you need help use the CD (track 38).
- Next say the sentence in four-part canon, as you did with the sentence above.

There's nothing like your favourite programme to cheer you up on a Sunday afternoon.

Forty-nine dirty leaves are sticking to my shoes; when Mum sees what a state I'm in she's going to blow a fuse!

71

Clapping in canon (teacher and children) (3, 4, 5, 6)

- In Year 3 only, rather than always clapping directly in front of you, clap the first set of four beats (or equivalent) to your right, the second set above your head, the third set to your left, and for the fourth set – pat your knees (instead of clapping).
- Below are some examples for you and the children to clap in canon. The speed, as well as the inclusion or otherwise of semiquavers will be factors in deciding the suitability of year group. To hear the two parts clearly, have the children patting their knees, which will contrast well with your clapping.
- Use the *Rhythm Patterns 1* or *3* sheets for further inspiration.

Clapping/playing percussion in canon (children only) (3, 4, 5, 6)

- As above, but have two, four, six, eight or more separate groups clapping or playing in canon. Always bring the first group in by clearly counting to 4 at the exact speed at which they should continue. At Year 6 level you might be able to hand the responsibility of improvising a canon to one of the pupils. This pupil will make up a 4-time clapping pattern as (s)he goes along.

Pre-arranged actions in canon (children only) (3, 4, 5, 6)

- Pre-arrange eight different actions in a certain order. First, all try out the actions, doing each one for four crotchet beats. You might want to go over some actions that can be carried out effectively and cleanly to a crotchet beat. For inspiration for actions take one part of the body and see how many different actions you can do with just that particular body part. With the arms there is considerable potential for inventing more actions if you consider household tasks, gardening tasks, playing instruments etc.
- Arrange the children in groups and try your actions in canon. The more groups and the faster the speed, the more difficult the activity. Use pop music as a backing track if you want but choose the track carefully to make sure the speed is appropriate for the year group.

Improvised actions in canon (children only) (4, 5, 6)

- Have one child inventing actions (4 crotchet beats per action) as they go along. (See above activity for action ideas.)

8, 4, 2, 1, 1 (3, 4, 5)

- Pre-decide eight different actions which can comfortably be carried out with a crotchet beat. See *Pre-arranged actions in canon* activity above for action ideas and bear in mind that something like a tick-tock head action is fine until it comes to doing a single one, which feels a bit peculiar.
- You play eight crotchet beats eight times on a percussion instrument while the children carry out the actions in the pre-arranged order, doing eight of each. Without a break change to a different percussion instrument.

Set the beat! (3, 4, 5, 6)

- This is a great game that can be enjoyed at many levels. The children should sit in a circle. One child – the 'guesser' – should go and hide his eyes. Meanwhile, choose a child from the circle who will be the 'beat-setter'. The other children must keep an eye on this child (and also an ear!) while not appearing to do so, and clap exactly what the beat-setter claps. The beat-setter should clap either crotchets or one of the other time values or a rhythm, such as:

- The guesser then returns and listens and watches. The beat-setter can change to a new beat/rhythm at any stage and the other children then immediately change too, but don't make the changes either too frantic or too infrequent. The guesser must try to work out who is the beat-setter. If you join in too, this will help iron out any inaccuracies of rhythm and so give the guesser a better chance of finding that beat-setter!

Code game (3)
- This game was introduced in Year 2 but there is plenty of scope for consolidation in Year 3. You will need a drum, a tambourine and a pair of claves.
- Ask the children to think about the sounds of their names. As a class work out which names sound the same – e.g. E-mi-ly Jack-son is the same as Har-ry Men-do-sa, but different from Me-lis-sa Green. Give the children practice at recognising their names. It will help if you say them with a strong rhythmic emphasis.
- The children should then arrange themselves in pairs or groups according to the sounds of their names. A few children might be alone. Those children in pairs should number themselves 1 and 2. Those in groups should number themselves 1, 2, 3 etc and remember their number.
- With the class list in front of you and the children remaining in the groups they have just formed, play the rhythm of any child's name on the **drum**. At this stage each child is trying to recognise whether this is the right sound for his/her name.
- If you have played the name of a child who is in a pair or a group, those children need to know exactly which child you have in mind. So next you should play the **tambourine** to give them another clue as to the name you are playing. If you play, for example, one tap, it signifies the first person of the group or pair. Two taps signifies the second, four taps will mean the fourth person (so this would mean someone from a larger group) and so on. If you don't play any taps on the tambourine then the children will have the added clue that it must be one of those children sitting on their own.
- Finally the **claves** tells the selected child where to run, according to the number of syllables you tap – one tap for door, two for cupboard etc. You can play up to five taps – or more if you want. You don't have to struggle to find a word with five syllables in your room – you could have, for example 'lots of co-loured balls'.

Right Royal Rap (3, 4, 5)
- Raps are great for feeling the beat. Using the lyric sheet, listen to the CD (track 39) to hear how to say the rap, then say it as a class with the backing track on the CD (track 40). Carefully count 8 steady beats before you come in. Inspired by track 40 you might like to create your own backing track.

Pig Rap (3, 4, 5)
- Using the lyric sheet, listen to the CD (track 41) to hear how to say the rap, then say it as a class with the backing track on the CD (track 42). Carefully count 8 steady beats before you come in.

Drum kit vocal exercises (6)
- In Lesson 1 of Year 6 (page 47) you will find the drum kit vocal exercise *Rock Beats*. Below are two examples of longer ones. They might inspire you to make up your own. Simply divide the class into four groups and

allocate a part to each group. The children should keep repeating their two-bar sound pattern, keeping in exact time throughout. Try it with the rap backing track (track 43) if you want.

1.

1	2	3	4	1	2	3	4
Boom	𝄽	*boom*	𝄽	*boom*	*boom*	𝄽	*boom*
tss	*tss tss*	*tss*	*tss tss*	*tss tss*	*tss*	*tss tss*	*tss*
doom	*doom*	*doom*	*doom*	*doom*	𝄽	*doodoom*	𝄽
ta-ka	*rok-ka*	*ra-ka*	*kra-ka*	𝄽	𝄽	*kraka*	*tak*

2.

1	2	3	4	1	2	3	4
Boom	*boom*	*boom*	𝄽	*boom*	𝄽	*boom*	𝄽
Tss tss	*rest*	*tss tss*	𝄽	𝄽	*tss*	*tss*	*tss*
Doom	*doom*	*doom*	*doo-doom*	*doom*	𝄽	𝄽	𝄽
Chaka	*tak*	𝄽	*tak*	𝄽	*taka*	*chaka*	*tak*

Drum kit hand and feet co-ordination exercises (5, 6)
- In Lesson 1 of Year 6 (page 47) we learnt a drum kit hand and feet co-ordination exercise. Here are two more. Some people like to get their hands co-ordinated first, and add the feet afterwards, and some prefer the other way round. (Try them at a dinner party at the end of the evening!)

  1. Hands alternate one tap each while feet alternate two.

  2. Feet alternate one tap each while hands alternate two.

Magic Cards (3)
- This appeared in the KS1 book but provides useful consolidation. Have roughly equal numbers of **crotchet**, **minim**, **quaver** and **semibreve** notation cards – enough for one each. Shuffle them so they are all mixed up. Give each child a card and ask them to sit in a large, spread-out circle so they can all see each other. Each child should look at his card in private, remember it, then put it face down on the floor beside him.
- Explain that you will be playing a steady crotchet beat on the drum throughout the activity, so those children with crotchets should simply clap the same beat as you. The other children should clap their respective beats to fit in. The object of the exercise is for the cards to magically group themselves so that *like* cards finish up together. This is what happens:
- At a given signal from you, all the children start to clap the beat indicated on their card while looking round the circle to see if they can spot anyone clapping the same beat. When they spot someone they immediately go to that person with their card, which they don't reveal. The two children leave their cards face down on the floor, stand up and continue to clap together. Meanwhile other groups will be starting to form in the same way. The sitting-down children can then look at the standing-up children and see which group they should join. When everyone has joined a group, reveal the cards.

Revealing the cards!

Magic Cards with semiquavers (5, 6)

- Play the game exactly as above but include semiquavers to make five groups. NB the crotchet pulse that you play on the drum will need to be slow enough to accommodate semiquavers.

Magic Cards with rhythms (4, 5, 6)

- Using the *Magic Cards* sheet, make a set of cards with one of three different rhythms on each instead of just a single beat. First, the children need to be sure of how to clap all these rhythms. Then distribute them randomly and the game works in exactly the same way as the games above, but don't have more than three rhythms in a game.
- This is a great game and a real test of children's ability to keep in time, to look and listen, to understand how notation works and maintain a rhythm despite other rhythms happening at the same time. Because it is such a popular game I have written out four games worth of rhythms! You can also invent your own.

3. Pitch work and songs

Sol-fa pitching practice (3, 4, 5, 6)

- To 'warm up' children's voices and to develop their pitch sense, simply work in the same way as you have done in the set lessons.

The Pitch Game (3, 4)

- This was introduced in Year 3 lesson 4. Try the remaining examples on track 6. The answers to all 10 are on page 19.

The interval game (6)

- First get used to the sound of each **interval** (distance between two notes) in the following way. Play C and then D on a pitched percussion instrument such as a glockenspiel. The class should practise singing these two consecutive notes to the word 'Hur' rather than 'la' (to avoid confusion with the **sol-fa** sound). C - D is a **step up**. D – C is a **step down**.
- Practise singing the following intervals in the same way:
  Skip or **3rd** = C – E
  Flea jump or **4th** = C – F
  Frog jump or **5th** = C – G
- Play random intervals and see if the children can recognise them.

Mix and Match

- You can make a team game out of this or, to make it more difficult, combine the aural activity with testing the knowledge of the notes on the stave. For this, give out copies of the *Blank Staves* sheet and ask the children to write down their responses by putting notes in the correct place on the stave.

Harmony Hits! – A game to extend pitch skills (6)
- You will need to prepare in advance a set of small cards or pieces of paper with one of the rhythms below written on each. Have roughly the same number of each rhythm
- Also write the two rhythms on the board.

- First work out how to clap each one as a class to be sure of the **rhythm**.
- Next try to work out, note by note, **interval** by **interval**, the tunes. If this proves difficult, *you* play the tunes on the glockenspiel. Remember C = do.
- Finally, practise the two tunes thoroughly as a class, then try half singing one while the other half sing the other at the same time.
- When you are sure everyone can accurately sing the sequences, randomly give out the cards/pieces of paper.
- The children should stand still in a space of their own looking at their respective tunes silently while you play each of the two starting notes on your glockenspiel and at the same time sing the relevant **sol-fa** sounds. This is everyone's opportunity to hum their first note and keep it in their heads. Now take a drum and tell the children you are going to play two lots of four steady crotchet beats, and then as you continue to keep the beat, the children should all sing what is on their paper. As they sing, they slowly move around the room and 'gather' anyone else who is also singing the same thing, until finally the class should form itself into two groups – each still singing its own rhythm.
- If the children are really up for a challenge, try the activity with three different rhythms. Below are six short melodies to provide more material.

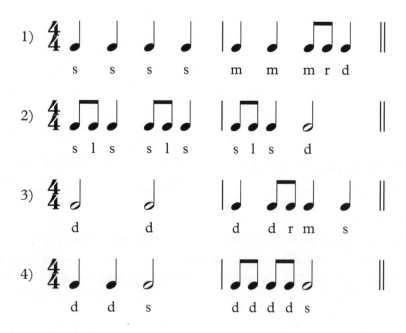

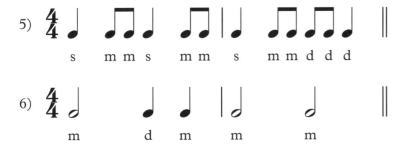

5) [musical notation] s m m s m m s m m d d d

6) [musical notation] m d m m m

Two songs at once (6)
- Give out copies of the sheet *Two songs at once*, or preferably use the OHP or whiteboard.
- It takes a great deal of focus to stay in tune for this activity. One of the tunes is already familiar to you, but the second one is not. It uses sounds from the sol-fa system to make sight reading it easier. First all try learning the second tune and singing it through together. Play the note C on a pitched instrument to start you off then try to sing without the help of the pitched instrument.
- Now divide the class into two groups. Play the notes G and the C below it, on a pitched instrument. These are the start notes for the two parts. Practise singing the two parts at the same time.
- You might like to sing with the backing track on the CD (track 43).

Plenty more songs for you to sing
The following songs and lyric sheets appear at the back of the book with the songs from the set lessons. They are also included on the ECD (CD2). Learn the songs with the help of the audio tracks.

Magic Spells (yr 3) (tracks 1 and 2)
Thread of my Dreams (yr 3) (tracks 3 and 4)
Spin the Straw (yr 4) (tracks 5 and 6)
Seasons Turn to Seasons (yr 4) (tracks 7 and 8)
The Greatest Gran of All (yr 5) (tracks 9 and 10)
Fire! (yr 5) (tracks 11 and 12)
The Disco Beat (yr 6) (tracks 13 and 14)
Rock 'n' Roll Boogie (yr 6) (tracks 15 and 16)

4. Improvising and composing
Stimuli
Pictures, poems stories and themes provide stimuli for improvisations and compositions (see Chapter 5, page X). Below is a list of ideas you can use as stimuli for composition. The first few give help, then you are on your own! Many of the themes/ideas suggested will be suitable for all four year groups because the children will work at their own level.

Instant improvisation with hand, mouth and body sounds (3, 4)
- Divide the class into four or more groups. Each group should pre-decide a random vocal or mouth noise. It is interesting here to note which noises made by the mouth are actually *vocal*. If you hum and put your hand on your throat you will hear your vocal chords resonating, so this is a vocal sound. If you say 'Sssh' with your hand on your throat you won't feel anything from your vocal chords so this is not a vocal noise. It's a good idea to investigate as many noises as possible before trying the activity.
- When you point to a group they should make their noise repeatedly. Unless you give them a signal to stop, they should carry on. In this way you can go in and out of different **timbres** and **textures** of sound, making a lovely sound collage. You might like to try this with specific noises, such as animal noises.
- Try mixing vocal/mouth sounds with body percussion sounds (clicking, clapping, tapping).
- You could also improvise with instruments. It doesn't matter whether the groups play rhythmically or just with a 'wash' of sound.
- A pupil could also take the part of the conductor.

Making a composition from the above improvisations (3, 4, 5, 6)
- Having heard how the various timbres and textures of the pre-decided vocal and/or percussive sounds work

together, sort out a precise structure for a piece – use the board if it helps – so the conductor doesn't simply point randomly at groups of children.

A set of three improvisations exploring the relationship between sound and silence

1. The teacher's gone! (no instruments required) (3)

- A very badly-behaved class of children has been told to keep quiet while the teacher leaves the classroom for a moment, but one or two start whispering, then gradually everyone is whispering, then some start to talk in normal voices, so the noise level continues to rise until everyone is shouting, at which point the teacher suddenly appears and claps his or her hands. Instantly there is silence.
- The children should sit in a circle. You 'conduct' the piece by slowly raising your hands from the floor to just above head level, at which point you clap. The floor represents silence. If you ask the children to simply whisper they don't know what to whisper so suggest whispering their names and addresses. They should whisper gently but quickly at first then get louder as they see your hand rising from the floor. When you clap they should immediately be silent. This gradual getting louder is called a **crescendo**. Notice how you left the silence gradually and re-entered it suddenly.

2. The show's over! (no instruments required) (3)

- Imagine the curtains closing at the end of a wonderful show and after a moment of silence the audience breaks into thunderous applause. The applause then gradually subsides until it dissolves into silence. This is called a **diminuendo**. Again, sitting in a circle, the children should watch you carefully as you 'conduct'. When you suddenly clap, that is the signal for everyone to start clapping very loudly. Keep your hands together on your own clap but then very slowly take them apart, just a chink at first then wider and wider until your arms are fully stretched out at the side. This action of yours will control the **diminuendo**. Finally, drop your head to signal complete silence. So in this improvisation the children are leaving silence suddenly and re-entering it gradually.

3. The thunderstorm (no instruments required) (3)

- Now the children are going to enter *and* leave silence gradually. Use the same way of controlling the volume as in *The teacher's gone!* So raise your hands slowly from the floor but then when the volume is at its highest begin to very slowly lower your hands again. The children should start by tapping just one or two fingers on the floor in front of them, then more fingers, gradually becoming louder, and then using hands, but make sure they are really listening and trying to control the **crescendo** so there are no sudden changes of volume. By the time your hand is at its highest they should be really beating the floor. The huge danger now is that the moment they see that your hand is starting to lower, they drop the volume suddenly. To avoid this, you might like to pre-decide that just one of the children will change from hand beating to finger tapping at this point and then go round the circle so that one at a time each of the other children also changes to fingers, then judge the last part of the **diminuendo** by decreasing the volume sensitively all together until your hand touches the ground and there is silence.

African drumming rhythms (4, 5, 6)

- This is a great activity to try out before listening to African drumming music, as recommended in the *Listening to music from other times and cultures* section. The more different types of drum, tambourine and shaker you have, the better.
- Ask a child to take any one of the above named instruments. Write the rhythms below up on the board and allocate one of them to this first child. Bring in four more children, one at a time, and allocate another of the rhythms to each of them so you are gradually building up a rhythmic collage. This is the 'demonstration' group; they should play their respective rhythms repeatedly and simultaneously.

- Rub the rhythms off the board. Divide the rest of the class into groups of five or six. What now follows will be head-bangingly noisy unless you have different areas in the school or in the playground where you are able to send groups of children. The **ensembles** (groups) are going to work out their own short piece using as many different rhythms as possible however they want, as long as there is a definite start and finish. You might be tempted to give more instruction than this, but try to resist the temptation. It's much better for the children to get to task. If you are obliged to remain in your one room, you might prefer to let one group at a time work with instruments while the others work on creating their different rhythms using the notation cards.

- When the groups all play their compositions to each other, this is the time to make positive comment about how creative and effective was each group's piece. You will probably be surprised at how the children instinctively incorporate dynamics and contrast in their pieces. It is also worth commenting on the value of the various approaches that the groups used in the preparation of their pieces. Some will have assigned or assumed a leader immediately, others will have a conductor, others might have prepared by simply taking turns, and others might have used their time badly, which will show!

- Now play the children some authentic African drumming music. You might find there is vocal/body sound added. Another effective element to a piece like this is movement/dance or some sort of visual impact about the way the ensemble is placed while playing.

- Send the groups off again to improve their pieces with the addition of one or more of these elements then re-appraise.

Chinese Pentatonic Music (5, 6)
- It is the use of the **Pentatonic** or five-note scale that gives Chinese music its distinctive quality.
- Try the following improvisation. One child should simply play the **ostinato** below on any pitched instrument (remember that **ostinato** implies continual repetition); and at the same time, another child should improvise a simple tune on piano, keyboard, xylophone or glockenspiel using the notes C D E G and A. You might like to add a shaker or guiro or another non-pitched percussion instrument of your choice.

- Take turns to produce Chinese pentatonic improvisations in small groups.

Train journey (3, 4, 5)
- Have four groups of instruments representing the train, the rain, the sun, the rainbow. There is huge scope for the train to stop and start, to speed up and slow down. The rain can also stop and start, get heavier and lighter. The sun might come out and go in again, or shine brightly or merely peep out from behind a cloud. It's up to you how you interweave these elements.

- See the list below for inspiration to work in the same way as for the *Train journey* piece to create other pieces.

Forest	Scarecrows
Forest fire	Music for an advertisement
Busy town centre	Party
Restaurant	Carnival
Kitchen of a restaurant	Fairground
Factory (think outside the box – what about a jumping bean factory?)	Circus
	Aliens
Ghosts dancing (could be comic)	Spinning wheel (think outside the box – what does it spin?)
Birds sighting and catching their prey	
Foxes scavenging	River – picking up and losing tributaries and finally going out to sea
Bin men	
Recycling plant	Fanfares
Supermarket check-out	Colours. Here are some ideas of emotions
Motor racing	associated with these colours:
Punch and Judy	Green – calm;
Argument	Yellow – happy, sunny;
Dinosaurs	Blue – sad;
On safari	Orange – strong;
Trolls	Red – angry;
Jungle Drums	Purple – peaceful;
Chinese Lanterns	Grey – bored

Mix and Match

5. Reading and writing music notation and graphic scores

All the exercises/activities below should inspire your own ideas along the same lines

Reading from two different kinds of graphic score (4, 5, 6)

1.
- In Year 4, Lesson 5, we worked on an accompaniment to the poem *Dustman's Drudge*, using **ostinati** written out very simply in an eight-beat format. At the back of the book/on the ECD you will find two sheets – *Two-bar blended ostinati* (Year 4) and *Four-bar blended ostinati* (Years 5 and 6), which work in the same way. Give out copies and work as a class or in groups.
- It is easy to make up patterns of sound and silence over eight beats. Try inventing some of your own.
- For a quick activity where you don't even have to get the instruments out, work out some blended ostinati along the same lines but with vocal sounds e.g. Shh, Pop, Tick, Brrr, Mm.

2.
- The other type of graphic score is where the squares are filled in with symbols representing sounds, and the time frame is much greater and looser, so instead of just eight or sixteen repeated beats of sounds and silence, there is a much more creative, expressive, less rhythmic sound result. Try working from the graphic scores *The Wind* and *Rampaging Robots* provided.

Writing your own graphic scores (4, 5, 6)
- Use the *Blank graphic score* sheet to create your own graphic scores following the guidelines laid down in Year 4, Lesson 2 (page 26).

Crotchets and rests to write on the board (3, 4)
- You clap any combination of crotchets and rests – just one bar in 4-time, and choose a child to try and write it on the board. (A wiggle will suffice for the rest!)
- Try the same thing but clap two bars this time:

e.g.

Crotchets, rests, semiquavers, and quavers to write on paper (5, 6)

- As above but make the rhythmic patterns more complex. Some one-bar and two-bar examples follow:

Crotchets and rests to write on paper (3, 4)

- You clap any combination of crotchets and rests – just one bar in 4-time. The children have to write down what you clap.
- Now try clapping two-bar rhythms. You might have to clap these more than once. Looking at the results will give you a strong idea of who has a good memory, a good sense of rhythm and an ability to discriminate aurally.

Hear the rhythm, see the rhythm (5, 6)

- This activity appeared in Year 3, Lesson 5 (page 22) in order to develop the joint skills of matching up the sound and sight of both rhythms and **sol-fa** notes. Here we are only focusing on matching the sound and sight of **rhythms**. Use the *Rhythm Patterns 3* sheet and carry out the activity as on page 22, omitting the **sol-fa** element.

Understanding dotted crotchets and single quavers (6)

- In Year 6, Lesson 5 (page 54) we briefly introduced the dotted crotchet. The sheet *Converting tied notes to dotted crotchets* provides consolidation of this concept. See the example below which shows how this is done. These two two-bar examples are rhythmically identical, but written out differently.

Musical words (5, 6)

- Give out copies of the *Musical words* sheet and see if the children can work out what words are formed by the given sequences of notes.

Seasons Turn to Seasons (5, 6)

- First listen to the song on CD2 (track 7).

Mix and Match

- Now give everyone a copy of the *Seasons Turn to Seasons* accompaniment sheet. Write a rough stave on the board and work out the notes of the **accompaniment** as a class, but don't make the mistake of writing the letters underneath the notes. There are five different notes involved in this accompaniment in all. Concentrate on the notes on the bottom three lines of the stave – E, G and B. The first three bars and the last bar are straightforward to work out, then move on to the middle four.
- Give pitched instruments out to no more than a third of the class, according to how many you have. Remember, if you have instruments with sixteen or more notes (i.e. two or more octaves) you can have two pupils per instrument.
- Now while two-thirds of the class sing through the song with the CD accompaniment (track 51), the third with instruments play the percussion accompaniment. Make sure everyone gets a turn at playing the accompaniment.
- Always appraise a performance. It might be that certain instruments simply don't sound good together, or there might be too many instruments to singers.

Twelve-bar Blues (6)
- Give out copies of the *Twelve-bar Blues* sheet, or preferably use the OHP or whiteboard.
- You will see that there are three parts to the piece and that the whole piece is twelve bars long. The pitch of the notes follows the traditional twelve-bar blues pattern. Work on the parts separately then try them altogether.
- You might like to invent some accompanying rhythms.

Play a round – *Spanish Inquisition* – getting used to sight-reading (6)
- As children's note reading skills improve they should be able to play pieces from sight, which means reproducing a piece reasonably accurately at first sight. The piece might involve pitch and rhythm or just rhythm. This is a great skill and one that will be so useful later in life.
- Divide the class into groups of eight. Each member of the group needs a copy of the *Spanish Inquisition* sheet. The piece should also be written on the board or projected on to a screen for the rest of the class to follow.
- Give instruments to just one group. Four children should have pitched percussion instruments (xylophones, glockenspiels or chime bar notes C, D, E, F, G, A, B, C), two should have tambourines and two, claves. At first the groups take turns to have a shot at sight-reading just eight bars of the piece. If everybody was to attempt the same eight bars, the last groups would have an unfair advantage, having heard the music so much that they might be able to simply play it by ear without reading the music. So I suggest that the first group attempts the first 2 lines, the second group, lines 2 and 3, the third group, lines 3 and 4, the fourth group, lines 4 and 1, the fifth, lines 1 and 2 etc.
- You should count the children in each time but then they must continue playing on the beat *no matter what happens*. This means that if they can't work out a pitched note quickly enough, they must leave it and keep following with their eyes in the hope that they might be able to join back in later. Those children not playing should listen to the other groups' efforts and make constructive criticism afterwards. Don't let any group have more than one attempt at the piece so that there is the minimum of 'waiting' time for children not playing.
- Each group should then have a second turn with members of the group playing different instruments.
- Now try in **canon** (a round). It is indicated on the music at what point the second, third and fourth players should start playing from the beginning. You might like to try it in two-part canon first then four-part.
- If you have more than four pitched instruments, organise the class accordingly.

You can play anything now!
- Well, not quite *any*thing, but now that the children can read music from the **treble clef** stave – i.e. notes from middle C to high G, a great deal of music will be open to them for playing on pitched percussion instruments and recorders with non-pitched additional parts.
- Pitched percussion instruments with loose bars for each note usually come with the additional black notes F sharp ♯ and B flat ♭. Don't be afraid of these black notes. If a piece requires an F♯ instead of an F, simply remove the F bar and put the F♯ bar in its place. If you are reading a piece of music where F sharps are required you will see the ♯ sign after the treble clef 𝄞 at the start of the piece. The note B flat works in exactly the same way. Look out for the flat ♭ sign at the start of the piece. If you see more than one sharp or flat at the start of a piece you will not be able to play the piece without additional black notes.

6. Listening to music from other times and cultures

Chapter 5 gives ideas for how to get the most out of classical, pop, jazz and world music as well as recommendations for getting hold of the music. Below is a list of short (under four minutes and often substantially under) classical pieces. If you are listening to a piece from a compilation CD, you might well feel more inspired by another piece on the CD than the one I have suggested, which is wonderful, of course! Equally, you might prefer to simply buy a couple of random compilations and use music from these, which is also fine, but do check the durations of the pieces as indicated on the back of the CD cover.

- 'Russian Dance' from *The Nutcracker* by Tchaikovsky
- *Sleigh Ride* K605, No. 3 by Mozart
- *Baby Elephant Walk* by Mancini
- *Celebration Overture* by Philip Lane
- 'March' from *The Nutcracker* by Tchaikovsky
- *The Syncopated Clock* by Leroy Anderson
- *March of the two left feet* by Leroy Anderson
- *Jazz Pizzicato* by Leroy Anderson
- *Love for Three Oranges* by Prokofiev
- *Hungarian Dance* No. 5 by Brahms
- 'In the Hall of the Mountain King' from *Peer Gynt* by Grieg
- *Pictures at an Exhibition* (A suite with fifteen short movements) by Mussorgsky
- *The Pines of the Villa Borghese* by Respighi
- *The Radetsky March* by Johann Strauss
- *Waltz of the Skaters* by Waldteufel
- 'Rondo-Allegro' from *Eine Kleine Nachtmusik* by Mozart
- 'Boisterous Bourrée' from *Simple Symphony* by Britten
- *Comedy Overture* by Adam Saunders
- *The Clog Dance* by Hérold
- 'The Comedian's Gallop' from *The Comedians* by Kabelevsky
- 'Dance of the Knights' from *Romeo and Juliet* by Prokoviev
- 'Can-can' from *Orpheus in the Underworld* by Offenbach
- *Sabre dance* by Khachaturian

Describe the music – a great team game (3, 4, 5, 6)
- Divide the class into two or three teams. Each child has a piece of paper and as the music is playing they must write down as many words and phrases to describe the music as they can. These words might include: fast, slow, high, low, loud, quiet, smooth, bouncy, thick texture, thin texture, sad, happy, sharp, rough, funny, scary, abrupt, watery, bright, dark, lonely, lively, upbeat, calm, chaotic, grand, passionate, fiery, gentle, deep, booming, silky, spiky, busy, dull, warm, cold, chilly, tinny, echoey, resounding, magical… The list goes on and on.
- At the end ask one child to read his list. Write on the board each *valid* word or phrase he has written. If the validity is in question, have a class discussion about it, but *you* make the final decision. The other children must cross off from their own lists any words or phrases as they appear on the board.
- Then ask a second child to read out any words from her list *which have not already been mentioned*. Add these to those words on the board and ask the other children to cross them off their lists. Make a note of any children who come up with a uniquely descriptive word or phrase.
- Continue like this until no-one has any more offerings. Give a point to the team of any child who came up with a valid unique answer, and see which team is the winner.

'Morning Mood' from *Peer Gynt* by Grieg (3, 4, 5, 6 – at your discretion)
- Start by considering the idea of circles and try out as many different types of circle as you can. Any part of your body can make a circle – hips, head, wrist(s), shoulders, elbows, feet. Hands and arms have countless possibilities from hands rolling over, to a finger drawing a cartwheel in the air, 'stirring the soup', being a helicopter blade.
- Now decide whether to start in a low, medium or high shape, facing the front, the back or the side and get into position.
- Put on the music and ask the children to move 'in slow motion' through as many different circles, large and small as they can think of, as smoothly as possible.

- To impose some shape on your movement piece, have four groups of children who take turns to move according to the **phrases** (musical sentences) in the music. You direct them, indicating that one group should 'freeze' and another begin to move whenever there seems to be a new section in the music.
- You might like to have a moment where all the children form a class circle and slowly walk round as if sleep walking and then gently 'dissolve' back into their own groups. Think of an equally effective ending. Maybe one child who is a particularly good mover might have a short solo and finish in the centre with everyone else making the same shape but at different levels.
- It is a bonus if your movement piece is visually inspiring, but is enough if it 'feels' good to the children involved.

More movement ideas (3, 4, 5, 6 – at your discretion)

- As the children are listening to the piece for the first time they should be imagining how to create a visual representation of it. Will the whole class be doing the same actions throughout, or will there be groups taking turns? What class shapes and patterns do they envisage?
- Remember you can work with the whole class in spaces doing the same thing, or with groups doing different things, or using just a walking action (in time to the beat, of course) and go in and out of different class shapes – a straight line, more than one straight line, a circle, groups of 2, 3 or 4 in set shapes etc.
- Below is a list of possible themes/ideas to inspire actions:
  push and pull
  circles
  contract and expand
  jobs around the house
  outside jobs
  playing instruments
  weather
  aliens
  patterns
  high, low, forwards, backwards
  sport

Jazz artists/composers to look out for on recordings:

Oscar Peterson	Arty Shaw
BB King	Dizzy Gillespie
John Lee Hooker	Charlie Parker
Louis Armstrong	Duke Ellington
Humphrey Littleton	Count Basie
Kenny Ball	Glen Miller
Benny Goodman	

Songs and other supplementary material

Chop Chop!

Words and music by Ann Bryant

CHORUS

Chop chop! goes the wood-cut-ter, Chop chop! goes the wood-cut-ter,

Chop chop! goes the wood-cut-ter, swing-ing his axe__ as he chops the wood.__

(last time) *Fine*

1. And the birds in the woods they

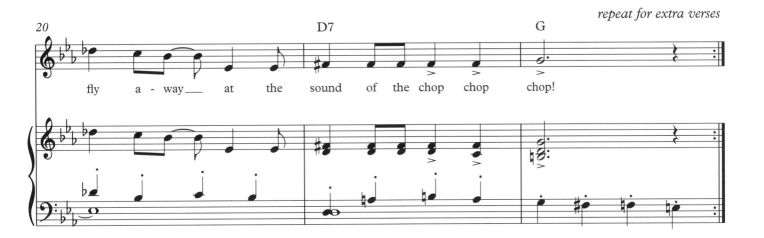

repeat for extra verses

Chop chop! goes the woodcutter,
Chop chop! goes the woodcutter,
Chop chop! goes the woodcutter,
Swinging his axe as he chops the wood.

1.   And the birds in the woods they fly away at the sound of the chop chop chop!
      The birds in the woods they fly away at the sound of the chop chop chop!

      Chorus

2.   And the mice in the woods they scurry away . . .

      Chorus

3.   And the rabbits in the woods they hop away . . .

      Chorus

4.   And the squirrels in the woods they scamper away . . .

      Chorus

5.   And the wolf in the woods he creeps away . . .

      Chorus

Songs

Magic Carpet

Words and music by Ann Bryant

Chorus (Part 1)
Sit me on a magic carpet,
Kit me out with giant wings,
Give me an engine, make me a sail,
And I can do a thousand things.

Chorus (Part 2)
What a strange place!   *What a strange place!*
Shall I go near?   *Shall I go near?*
What can I see?   *What can I see?*
What can I hear?   *What can I hear?*

1. There are snowflakes and diamonds tumbling from the sky.
    On the trees there are baby stars twinkling on high.
    And the houses are silver, the roses are green,
    So strange a place as this I'm sure I've never ever seen.

    Chorus (Parts 1 and 2)

2. There is music and dancing ev'rywhere you go,
    And the people are laughing, faces aglow,
    There is bright golden sunshine all mingling with the rain.
    So this is where the rainbow ends and where it starts again.

    Chorus (Part 1)

Songs

Now is Now

Words by Ann Bryant
Music by David Mitchener and Ann Bryant

When your world is like a tunnel and there's no light,
Keep walking onwards 'cause that way is always right.

Don't look back because you can't undo the past.
Nothing's for ever, no nothing can last.

Now is now and it's yours to keep.
Now is now, yours to give.
Now is now and it's yours to keep,
To dream, to sleep,
To live, because . . .

When your world is like a tunnel and there's no light,
Keep walking onwards 'cause that way is always right.

Don't forget we're only young, we've just begun.
Keep dreaming, keep working, keep having fun.

Sing an' Jump Up for Joy

Trad. Antigua
arr. Bolam/Gritton

Freedom an' dignity,
Freedom an' dignity.

This an' more have come to all our people.
Sing an' jump up for joy,
Sing an' jump up for joy,
Show the world that we are all one people.

Antigua, so beautiful!
Antigua, so wonderful!
Beaches plentiful, climate healthy,
People peaceable, life so lengthy,
Hospitality full an' plenty:
Antigua!

Songs

Magic Spells

Words and music by Ann Bryant

after verse 4
(all four groups say their words simultaneously as indicated)

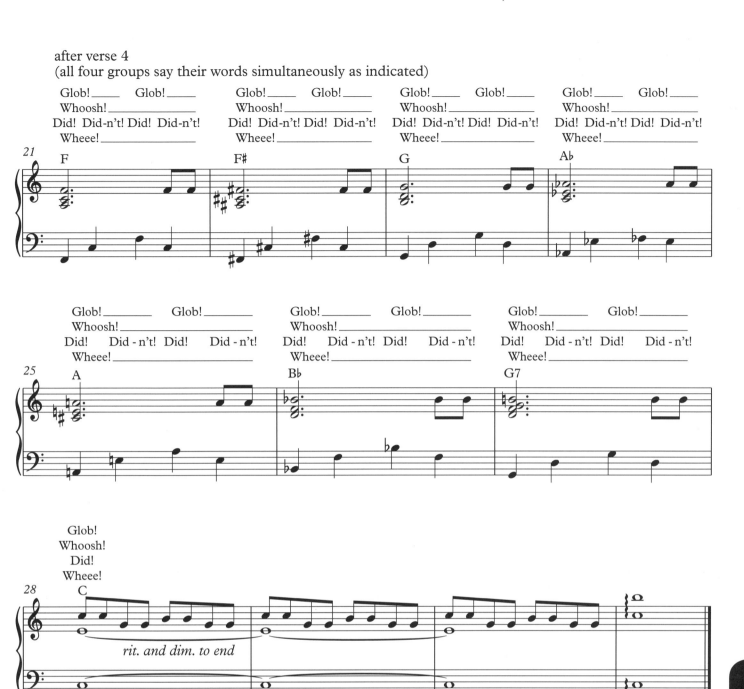

Magic I have done, since I was only one,
I can do it very well,
Take my silver wand, wave it in the air,
And now I say my spell.

1. Hocus pocus, give me izzy wizzy woo,
   Turn these children into globules of glue!
   Glob! Glob! Glob! Glob! Glob! Glob! Glob! Glob!

   Chorus

2. Hocus pocus, give me izzy wizzy wiz,
   Turn these children into nine pints of fizz!
   Whoosh! Whoosh! Whoosh! Whoosh!

   Chorus

3. Hocus pocus, give me izzy wizzy wow,
   Turn these children into one blazing row!
   Did! Didn't! Did! Didn't! Did! Didn't! Did! Didn't!

   Chorus

4. Hocus pocus, give me izzy wizzy whee,
   Turn these children into Ferdinand the Flea!
   Wheee! Wheee! Wheee! Wheee!

(All four groups say their words simultaneously till end)

Thread of my Dreams

Words and music by Ann Bryant

Songs

1. Soft as a whis-per the mist of the dawn, As I o-pen my eyes to an-

-o -ther new day. Si - lent and still is the world so it seems.

Gent - ly I tread on the thread of my dreams, Sum - mer is

slip - ping and slid - ing and glid - ing a - way.

1. Soft as a whisper the mist of the dawn,
    As I open my eyes to another new day.
    Silent and still is the world so it seems.
    Gently I tread on the thread of my dreams,
    Summer is slipping and sliding and gliding away.

2. Gossamer cobwebs are heavy with dew,
    Soft falling leaves but there's no other sound.
    Dead and laid bare is the earth so it seems.
    Gently I tread on the thread of my dreams,
    Yes, there are stories to tell from the world underground.

3. Seeds that were sown long ago in the deep
    Are the harvest of flowers and fruit for today.
    Beauty and colour abound so it seems.
    Gently I tread on the thread of my dreams,
    Safely we gather together and 'Thank you' we say.

Songs

Spin the Straw

Words and music by Ann Bryant

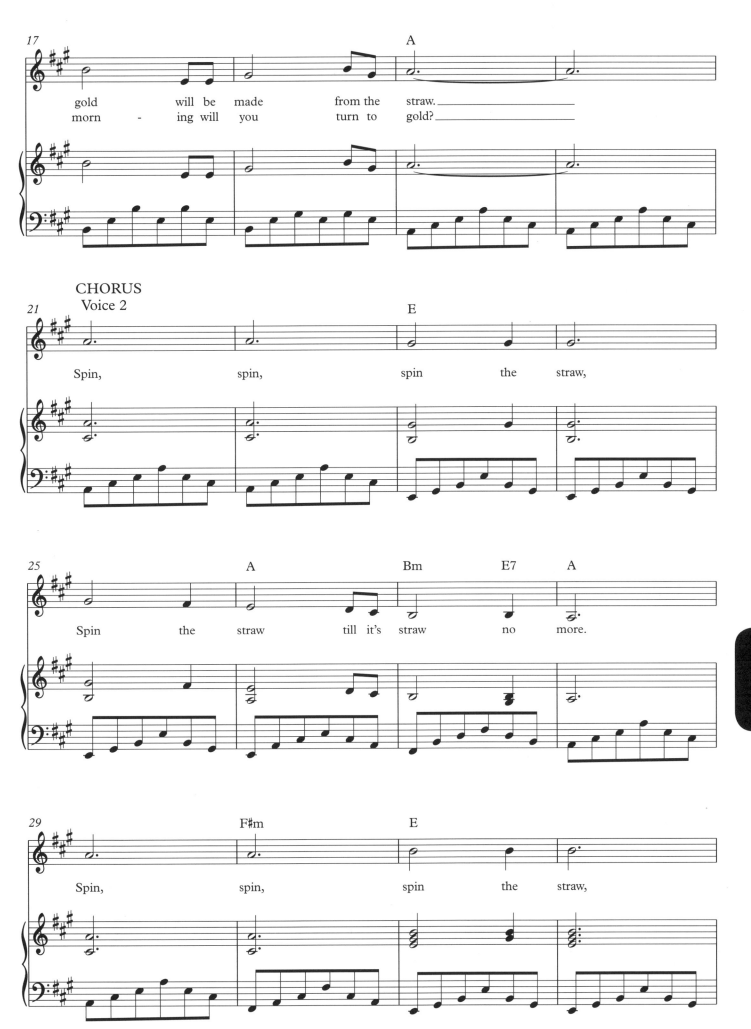

1. If I try and I try with all my might,
    If I work till my fingers are sore,
    If I spin and I twist and I pray all night,
    Maybe gold will be made from the straw.

    Spin, spin, spin the straw,
    Spin the straw till it's straw no more.
    Spin, spin, spin the straw,
    Spin the straw into gold.

2. Can you hear, can you hear, can you hear me straw?
    Will you try to do as you're told?
    If I spin and I twist and I pray all night
    In the morning will you turn to gold?

    Chorus

3. *Verse 1 and Chorus sung at the same time*

Seasons Turn to Seasons

Words and music by Ann Bryant

1. Sea-sons turn to sea-sons and the years go by. Seed is scat-tered in the fields so bare. The buds be-gin to turn to flow-ers, High and low the col-ours show, And spring is smil-ing good-ness ev-'ry-where.

1. Seasons turn to seasons and the years go by.
    Seed is scattered in the fields so bare.
    The buds begin to turn to flowers,
    High and low the colours show,
    And spring is smiling goodness ev'rywhere.

2. Seasons turn to seasons and the years go by.
    Everything is tall and green and good.
    The shining sun that filters through
    The thickly laden boughs; it's true
    That summer's on the hill and in the wood.

3. Seasons turn to seasons and the years go by.
    Reaping in the fields of corn and wheat.
    The apples from the trees in baskets,
    Marrows from the fields in trugs,
    The harvest of our autumn here to eat.

4. Seasons turn to seasons and the years go by.
    Hands upon the plough to turn the earth.
    The wood is sawn and stacked and sawn
    To make the fires that keep us warm,
    And winter tells the Christmas story's birth.

The Greatest Gran of All

Words and music by Ann Bryant

1. My great gran just a - dores trea - cle flan,__ says ba - na - nas and bran__ are for
2. My great gran has a bril - li - ant plan,__ runs as fast as she can__ when she

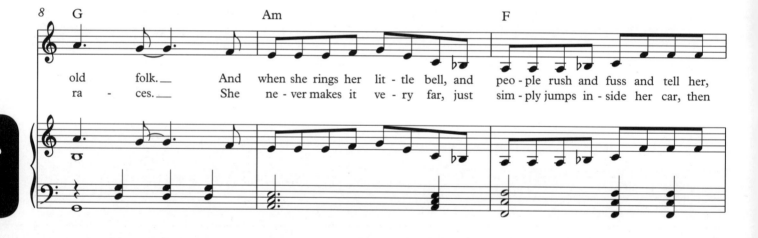

old folk.__ And when she rings her lit - tle bell, and peo - ple rush and fuss and tell her,
ra - ces.__ She ne - ver makes it ve - ry far, just sim - ply jumps in - side her car, then

'Care - ful, Gran! Don't o - ver - do it!' Gran says, 'What a__ joke!'
at the end, runs round the bend, and says, 'I'm__ such a__ star!'

1. My great gran just adores treacle flan,
    Says banana and bran are for old folk.
    And when she rings her little bell,
    And people rush and fuss and tell her,
    'Careful, Gran! Don't overdo it!'
    Gran says, 'What a joke!'

    Chorus
    Whatever she does, however she does it,
    Whatever she does, however she does it,
    She's the greatest gran, she's the greatest gran,
    She's the greatest gran of all!

2. My great gran has a brilliant plan,
    Runs as fast as she can when she races.
    She never makes it very far,
    Just simply jumps inside her car,
    Then at the end, runs round the bend,
    And says, 'I'm such a star!'

    Chorus

105

Fire!

Words and music by Ann Bryant

Steady, rhythmic

1. Flick - er, flick - er, flick - er, flick - er.

Smoke is curl - ing thick - er, fire is grow - ing quick - er, And the ti - ni - est flame___ licks a

lit - tle bit fur - ther, Spread - ing the fire___ just a lit - tle bit more. And the

flames climb up high___ and the sparks start to fly,___ And the smoke fills the sky.___ It's the

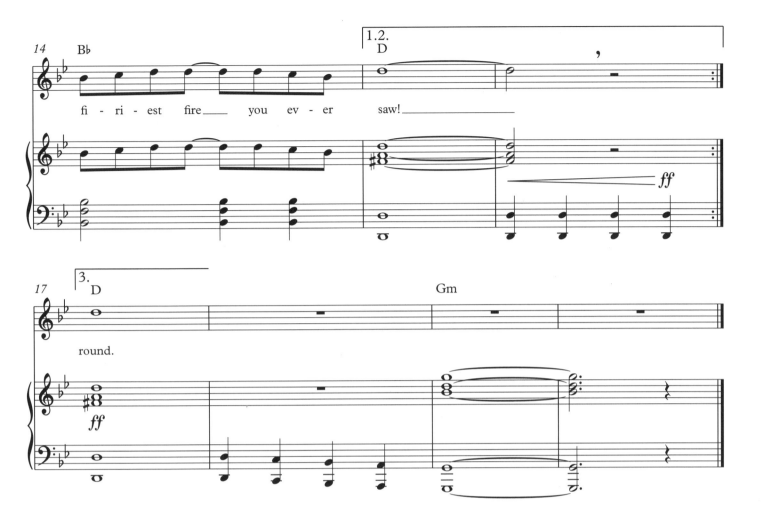

1. Flicker, flicker, flicker, flicker.
   Smoke is curling thicker, fire is growing quicker,
   And the tiniest flame licks a little bit further,
   Spreading the fire just a little bit more.
   And the flames climb up high and the sparks start to fly,
   And the smoke fills the sky.
   It's the firiest fire you ever saw!

2. Nee Naw, Nee Naw, Nee Naw, Nee Naw*.
   Coming to our aid from the fire brigade
   Is the smallest red dot getting bigger and bigger,
   Closer and closer, its sirens a-blare.
   And the great hoses swoop and the jets loop the loop
   And the flames stretch and stoop
   There's a fire-water soup in the air!

3. Water, water, water, water,
   Wet it, wash it, squirt it, jet it, splosh it, spurt it,
   Till the last little flame says goodbye to the world,
   Cinders like flakes, soft and black on the ground.
   And the sky that was bright, turns to grey what was white,
   Turns to dark what was light,
   As the shadows of night gather around!

*Imitating fire engine siren

The Disco Beat

Words and music by Lin Marsh

1. There's a song in my heart and a rhythm in my feet,
    Gonna sing and dance to the disco beat.
    I can feel it in my fingers, feel it in my toes,
    It's the one way of moving that ev'ryone knows.

    Chorus
    So move with the beat, feel that syncopation,
    Move those feet, what's the hesitation?
    Leave those cares and worries behind,
    Get with the music, let your body unwind.

2. Do you feel in the mood, are you ready to begin?
    Shake your body loose as the lights grow dim.
    Hear the music all around you, moving you along,
    Let your feet take you dancing and join in our song.

    Chorus

Songs

Rock 'n' Roll Boogie

Words and music by David Mitchener

111

1. Come to the club,
   Come and hear some boogie blues.
   Join the queue,
   Soon we'll have you tappin' your toes.
   Get on board,
   We'll take you on a musical cruise.

   Chorus
   Down and cool,
   We do the rock 'n' roll boogie.
   After school,
   We sing a song of swing and jazz and blues and boogie woogie.

2. Join the band,
   Come and blow the blues away.
   Get on the plane,
   Fly us to the place to play.
   Feel the groove,
   Pumpin' through you ev'ry day.

   Chorus

   Boogie woogie!
   Come and do the rock 'n' roll boogie woogie.
   Boogie woogie!

   Repeat verse 1 and chorus to end

Chop Chop!   by Ann Bryant

Chorus
Chop chop! goes the woodcutter,
Chop chop! goes the woodcutter,
Chop chop! goes the woodcutter,
Swinging his axe as he chops the wood.

1. And the birds in the woods they fly away
        at the sound of the chop chop chop!
   The birds in the woods they fly away
        at the sound of the chop chop chop!

   Chorus

2. And the mice in the woods they scurry away…

   Chorus

3. And the rabbits in the woods they hop away…

   Chorus

4. And the squirrels in the woods they scamper away…

   Chorus

5. And the wolf in the woods he creeps away…

   Chorus

Lyric Sheets

Magic Carpet   Ann Bryant

Chorus (Part 1)
Sit me on a magic carpet,
Kit me out with giant wings,
Give me an engine, make me a sail,
And I can do a thousand things.

Chorus (Part 2)
What a strange place!   *What a strange place!*
Shall I go near?   *Shall I go near?*
What can I see?   *What can I see?*
What can I hear?   *What can I hear?*

1. There are snowflakes and diamonds tumbling from the sky.
   On the trees there are baby stars twinkling on high.
   And the houses are silver, the roses are green,
   So strange a place as this I'm sure I've never ever seen.

Chorus (Parts 1 and 2)

2. There is music and dancing ev'rywhere you go,
   And the people are laughing, faces aglow,
   There is bright golden sunshine all mingling with the rain.
   So this is where the rainbow ends and where it starts again.

Chorus (Part 1)

Now is Now   Ann Bryant and David Mitchener

1. When your world is like a tunnel and there's no light,
    Keep walking onwards 'cause that way is always right.
    Don't look back because you can't undo the past.
    Nothing's for ever, no nothing can last.

    Now is now and it's yours to keep.
    Now is now, yours to give.
    Now is now and it's yours to keep,
    To dream, to sleep,
    To live, because …

2. When your world is like a tunnel and there's no light,
    Keep walking onwards 'cause that way is always right.
    Don't forget we're only young, we've just begun
    Keep dreaming, keep working, keep having fun.

Lyric Sheets

Sing an' Jump Up for Joy

Trad.

Freedom an' dignity,
Freedom an' dignity.
This an' more have come to all our people.
Sing an' jump up for joy,
Sing an' jump up for joy,
Show the world that we are all one people.

Antigua. So beautiful!
Beaches plentiful, climate healthy,
People peaceable, life so lengthy,
Hospitality full an' plenty: Antigua!

Antigua. So wonderful!
Beaches plentiful, climate healthy,
People peaceable, life so lengthy,
Hospitality full an' plenty: Antigua!

Lyric
Sheets

Magic Spells   Ann Bryant

Chorus
Magic I have done, since I was only one,
I can do it very well,
Take my silver wand, wave it in the air,
And now I say my spell.

1. Hocus pocus, give me izzy wizzy woo,
   Turn these children into globules of glue!
   Glob! Glob! Glob! Glob! Glob! Glob! Glob! Glob!

Chorus

2. Hocus pocus, give me izzy wizzy wiz,
   Turn these children into nine pints of fizz!
   Whoosh! Whoosh! Whoosh! Whoosh!

Chorus

3. Hocus pocus, give me izzy wizzy wow,
   Turn these children into one blazing row!
   Did! Didn't! Did! Didn't! Did! Didn't! Did! Didn't! (x2)

Chorus

4. Hocus pocus, give me izzy wizzy whee,
   Turn these children into Ferdinand the Flea!
   Wheee! Wheee! Wheee! Wheee!

(All four groups say their words simultaneously till end)

Lyric Sheets

Thread of my Dreams by Ann Bryant

1. Soft as a whisper the mist of the dawn,
   As I open my eyes to another new day.
   Silent and still is the world so it seems.
   Gently I tread on the thread of my dreams,
   Summer is slipping and sliding and gliding away.

2. Gossamer cobwebs are heavy with dew,
   Soft falling leaves but there's no other sound.
   Dead and laid bare is the earth so it seems.
   Gently I tread on the thread of my dreams,
   Yes, there are stories to tell from the world underground.

3. Seeds that were sown long ago in the deep
   Are the harvest of flowers and fruit for today.
   Beauty and colour abound so it seems.
   Gently I tread on the thread of my dreams,
   Safely we gather together and 'Thank you' we say.

Lyric Sheets

Spin the Straw   Ann Bryant

1. If I try and I try with all my might,
   If I work till my fingers are sore,
   If I spin and I twist and I pray all night,
   Maybe gold will be made from the straw.

   Chorus
   Spin, spin, spin the straw,
   Spin the straw till it's straw no more.
   Spin, spin, spin the straw,
   Spin the straw into gold.

2. Can you hear, can you hear, can you hear me straw?
   Will you try to do as you're told?
   If I spin and I twist and I pray all night
   In the morning will you turn to gold?

   Chorus

3. *Verse 1 and Chorus sung at the same time*

Lyric Sheets

Seasons Turn to Seasons   Ann Bryant

1. Seasons turn to seasons and the years go by.
   Seed is scattered in the fields so bare.
   The buds begin to turn to flowers,
   High and low the colours show,
   And spring is smiling goodness ev'rywhere.

2. Seasons turn to seasons and the years go by.
   Everything is tall and green and good.
   The shining sun that filters through
   The thickly laden boughs; it's true
   That summer's on the hill and in the wood.

3. Seasons turn to seasons and the years go by.
   Reaping in the fields of corn and wheat.
   The apples from the trees in baskets,
   Marrows from the fields in trugs,
   The harvest of our autumn here to eat.

4. Seasons turn to seasons and the years go by.
   Hands upon the plough to turn the earth.
   The wood is sawn and stacked and sawn
   To make the fires that keep us warm,
   And winter tells the Christmas story's birth.

The Greatest Gran of All

Ann Bryant

1. My great Gran just adores treacle flan
   Says bananas and bran are for old folk.
   And when she rings her little bell
   And people rush and fuss and tell her,
   'Careful, Gran! Don't over do it!'
   Gran says, 'What a joke!'

   Chorus
   Whatever she does, however she does it,
   Whatever she does, however she does it,
   She's the greatest Gran, she's the greatest Gran,
   She's the greatest Gran of all!

2. My great Gran has a brilliant plan,
   Runs as fast as she can when she races.
   She never makes it very far,
   Just simply jumps inside her car,
   Then at the end, runs round the bend,
   And says, 'I'm such a star!'

   Chorus

Lyric Sheets

Fire!   Ann Bryant

1. Flicker, flicker, flicker, flicker.
   Smoke is curling thicker, fire is growing quicker,
   And the tiniest flame licks a little bit further,
   Spreading the fire just a little bit more.
   And the flames climb up high and the sparks start to fly,
   And the smoke fills the sky.
   It's the firiest fire you ever saw!

2. Nee Nah, Nee Nah, Nee Nah, Nee Nah.
   Coming to our aid from the fire brigade
   Is the smallest red dot getting bigger and bigger,
   Closer and closer, its sirens a-blare.
   And the great hoses swoop and the jets loop the loop
   And the flames stretch and stoop
   There's a fire-water soup in the air!

3. Water, water, water, water,
   Wet it, wash it, squirt it, jet it, splosh it, spurt it,
   Till the last little flame says goodbye to the world,
   Cinders like flakes, soft and black on the ground.
   And the sky that was bright, turns to grey what was white,
   Turns to dark what was light,
   As the shadows of night gather around!

The Disco Beat

Lin Marsh

1. There's a song in my heart and a rhythm in my feet,
   Gonna sing and dance to the disco beat.
   I can feel it in my fingers, feel it in my toes,
   It's the one way of moving that ev'ryone knows.

   Chorus
   So move with the beat, feel that syncopation,
   Move those feet, what's the hesitation?
   Leave those cares and worries behind,
   Get with the music, let your body unwind.

2. Do you feel in the mood, are you ready to begin?
   Shake your body loose as the lights grow dim.
   Hear the music all around you, moving you along,
   Let your feet take you dancing and join in our song.

   Chorus

Lyric Sheets

Rock 'n' Roll Boogie   David Mitchener

1. Come to the club,
   Come and hear some boogie blues,
   Join the queue,
   Soon we'll have you tappin' your toes.
   Get on board,
   We'll take you on a musical cruise.

   Chorus
   Down and cool,
   We do the rock and roll boogie.
   After school,
   We sing a song of swing and jazz and blues and boogie woogie,
   Yeah!

2. Join the band,
   Come and blow the blues away!
   Get on the plane,
   Fly us to the place to play.
   Feel the groove,
   Pumpin' through you every day.

   Chorus

   Boogie! Woogie!
   Come and do the rock 'n' roll boogie woogie!
   Boogie! Woogie!

   Repeat verse 1 and chorus

Lyric Sheets

Right Royal Rap!   Ann Bryant

1. *KING:*

   Well, the spade's in the bucket and the bucket holds the spade
   But it's me who made the kingdom like the kingdom is made.
   QUEEN:
   Yeah, the spade's in the bucket and the bucket holds the spade
   But it's *me* who made the kingdom like the kingdom is made.

   Chorus
   With a hip and a hop and a hip hop hap
   We're giving you all the right royal rap

2. *KING:*

   Well, you can't beat love, cos your heart beats good
   Yeah your heart beat beats like a royal heart should.
   QUEEN:
   No, you can't beat love, cos your heart beats good
   Yeah your heart beat beats like a royal heart should.

   Chorus

3. *KING:*

   Well, diamonds are forever, they're forever a gem,
   And the King and the Queen, we've got plenty of them.
   QUEEN:
   Yeah, we sparkle and we shimmer from our head to our toes
   And we glisten and we glimmer wherever we goes!

   Chorus

4. *KING:*

   Well this is a club you've just gotta be in
   Cos this is the club where all clubs begin.
   QUEEN:
   There's a club for the King, there's a club for the Queen,
   Yeah, come and visit club land for a swinging scene.

   Chorus

Lyric Sheets

Pig Rap

Ann Bryant

Chorus
I'm a pig. Yo! And I live in a pen.
Cos I'm a pig. Yo! You can say that again.

1. You see us pigs down and dirty and we roll in the mud,
   Ain't never chewin' the cud, man. No! Man!

Chorus

2. You see us rockin' on our trotters and we're bringin' the beat,
   Ain't never hot in the hear, man. No! Man!

Chorus

3. You see us packin' back the pickings of the greatest o' grub,
   Ain't never scared of the blub, man. No! Man!

Chorus

Cos I'm a pig! Yo! Yo!

Note Value Cards

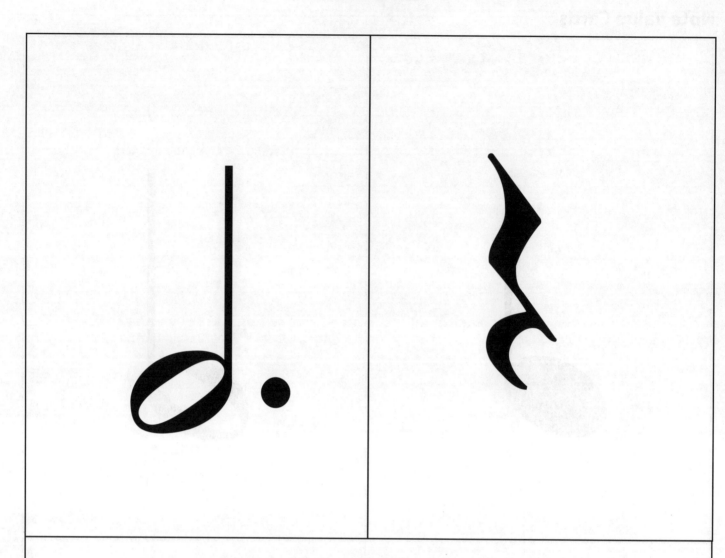

Pupils' Sheets

Sol-fa Hand Signs

DO   RE   MI

FA   SO   LA

TI   high DO

Rhythm Patterns 1 (in 4-time)

Dustman's Drudge graphic score

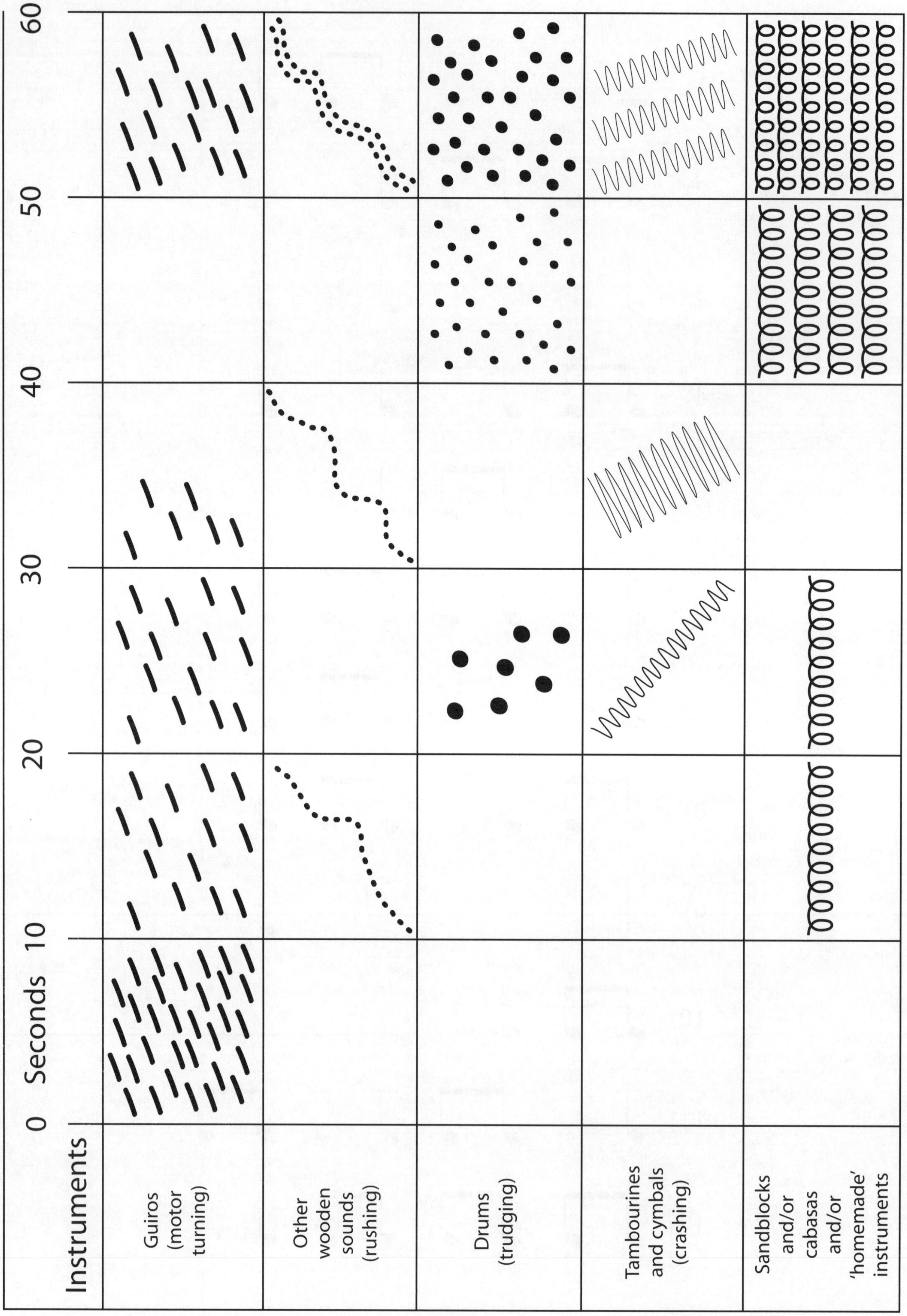

Blank Graphic Score

Instruments				

0   Seconds

Rhythm Patterns 2

Steps

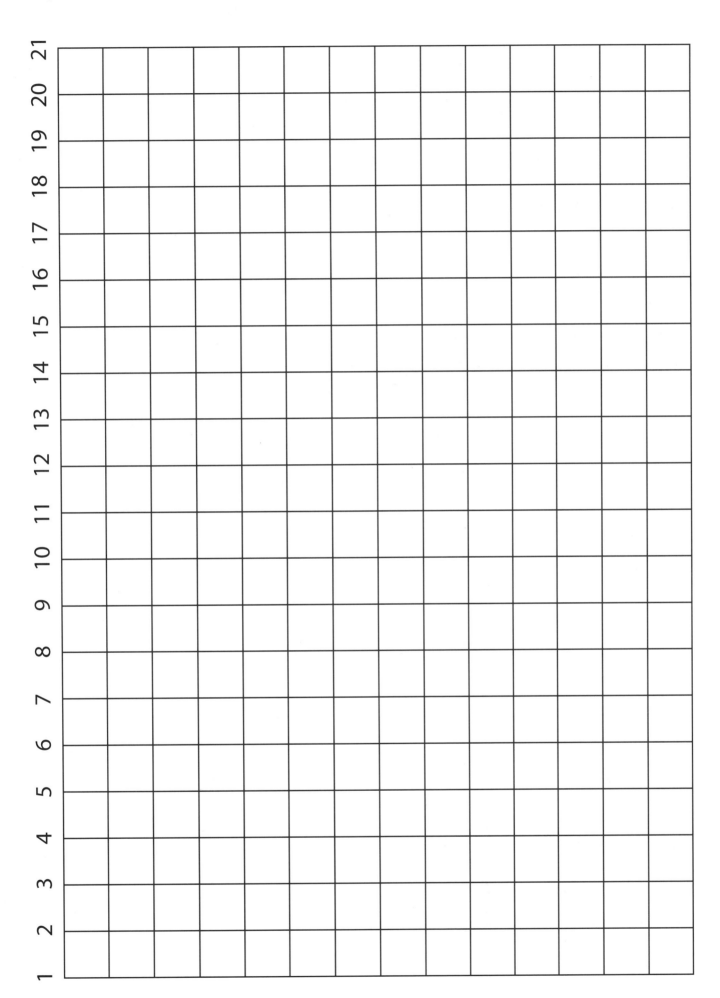

Dustman's Drudge accompaniment

Words / Instruments	1	2	3	4	5	6	7	8
Words	Mo -	tor	turn -	ing	Mo -	tor	turn -	ing
	Jump - ing	from the	van	and	rush - ing	to the	bin.	
	Heave	it	high	then	trudge	with	drudg - er -	y
	Fix it	on	the	and	tip it	all	in.	
	Crash -	ing	crunch -	ing	grat -	ing	munch -	ing
	Churn -	ing	rub - bish	in a	splat - ter -	ton - ic	spin.	
Tambourines	⊕			⊕	⊕			⊕
Claves		✗		✗		✗	✗	
Finger cymbals	◠		◠		◠			
Shakers	⚲	⚲	⚲		⚲		⚲	

136

Semiquaver Patterns (in 4-time)

1)

1 and 2 and 3 and 4 and   1 and 2 and 3 and 4 and

2)

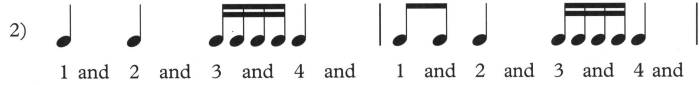

1 and 2 and 3 and 4 and   1 and 2 and 3 and 4 and

3)

1 and 2 and 3 and 4 and   1 and 2 and 3 and 4 and

4)

1 and 2 and 3 and 4 and   1 and 2 and 3 and 4 and

1 and 2 and 3 and 4 and   1 and 2 and 3 and 4 and

1 and 2 and 3 and 4 and   1 and 2 and 3 and 4 and

1 and 2 and 3 and 4 and   1 and 2 and 3 and 4 and

1 and 2 and 3 and 4 and   1 and 2 and 3 and 4 and

Blank Staves

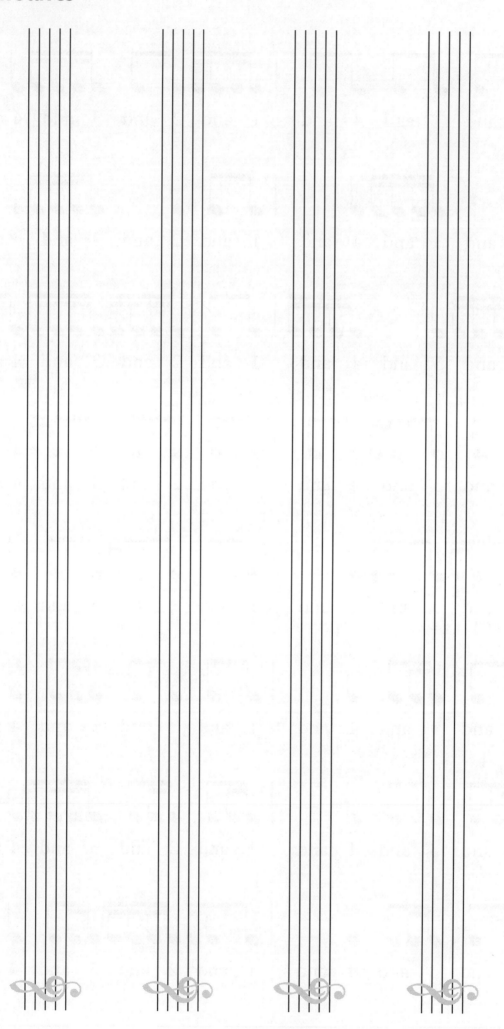

138

Syncopated shopping

Class clap and say:

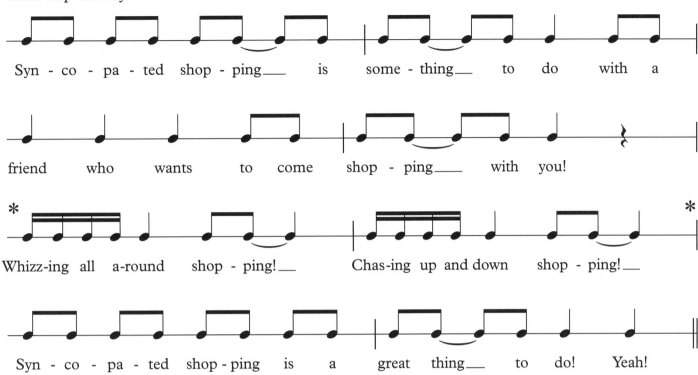

Syn - co - pa - ted shop - ping___ is some - thing___ to do with a

friend who wants to come shop - ping___ with you!

* Whizz-ing all a-round shop - ping!___ Chas-ing up and down shop - ping!___ *

Syn - co - pa - ted shop - ping is a great thing___ to do! Yeah!

* The bars between asterisks should be played on a solo percussion instrument the first time through. Play the piece through five times, substituting one of the two-bar rhythms below after the first play-through.

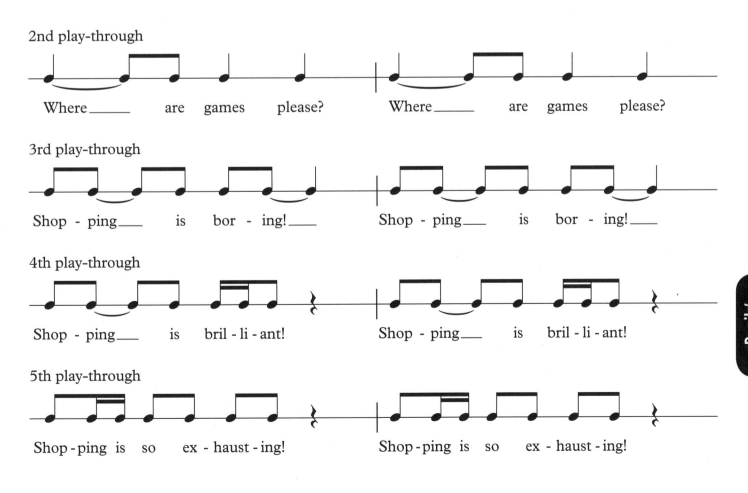

2nd play-through

Where_____ are games please? Where_____ are games please?

3rd play-through

Shop - ping___ is bor - ing!___ Shop - ping___ is bor - ing!___

4th play-through

Shop - ping___ is bril - li - ant! Shop - ping___ is bril - li - ant!

5th play-through

Shop - ping is so ex - haust - ing! Shop - ping is so ex - haust - ing!

This Old Man

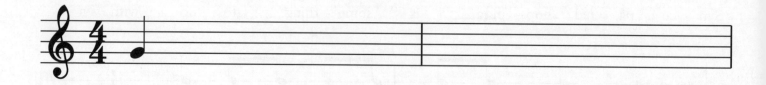

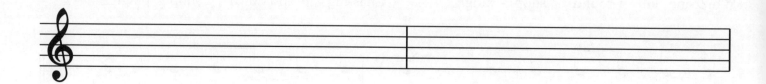

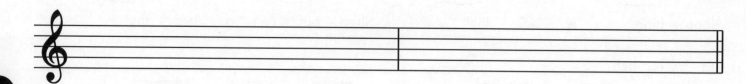

Rhythm Patterns 3

1)

2)

3)

4)

5)

6)

7)

8)

9)

10)

11)

12)

Two songs at once

Two-bar blended ostinati

Four-bar blended ostinati

Graphic Score – *The Wind*

	5 Drums on floor, played with fingertips	5 Hand Drums, scraped	5 Sand blocks	5 Wood blocks	5 Scrapers or Guiros
Wind has gone and all is calm					
Wind is really causing havoc					
Rain and leaves are swirling, whirling					
Branches creaking branches creaking					
Shutters banging shutters banging					
Leaves are rustling leaves are rustling					
Wind is stirring wind is stirring					
Raindrops falling raindrops falling					

Graphic Score – *Rampaging Robot*

Converting tied notes to dotted crotchets

(we have begun the first example for you)

Musical Words

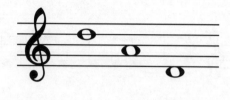

B E D

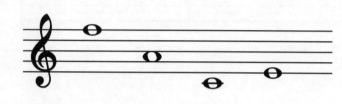

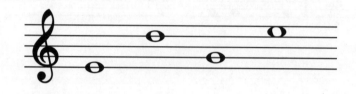

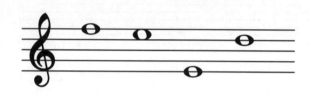

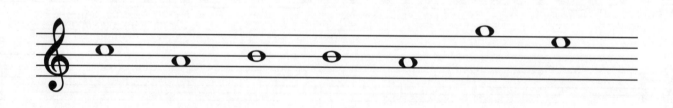

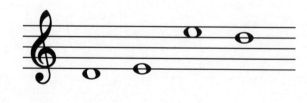

Seasons Turn to Seasons accompaniment

accomp.

Sea - sons turn to sea - sons and the years go by

accomp.

accomp.

accomp.

Twelve-bar Blues

Spanish Inquisition

treble clef (see glossary)

* second part starts piece at this point

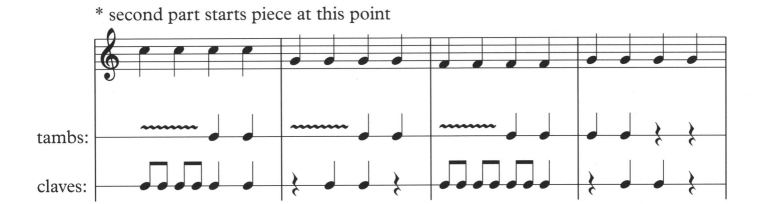

* third part starts piece at this point

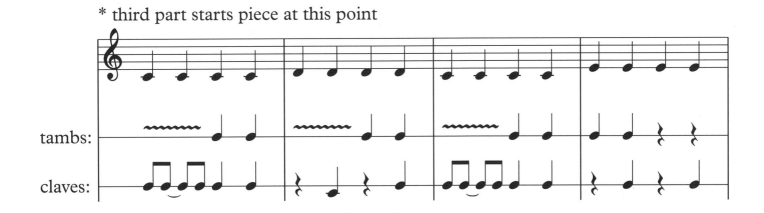

* fourth part starts piece at this point

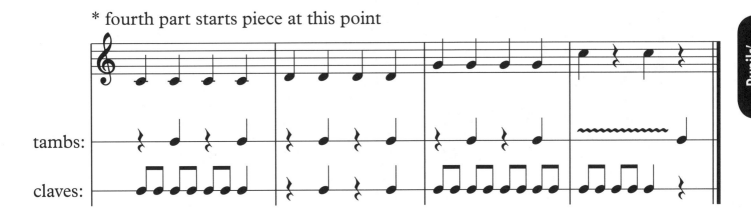

Magic Cards

National Curriculum for England
Key Stage 2 – Music

Knowledge, skills and understanding

Teaching should ensure that **listening,** and **applying knowledge and understanding,** are developed through the interrelated skills of **performing, composing** and **appraising.**

Controlling sounds through singing and playing – performing skills
1. Pupils should be taught how to:
   a) Sing songs, in unison and two parts, with clear diction, control of pitch, a sense of phrase and musical expression
   b) play tuned and untuned instruments with control and rhythmic accuracy
   c) practice, rehearse and present performances with an awareness of the audience

Creating and developing musical ideas – composing skills
2. Pupils should be taught how to:
   a) improvise, developing rhythmic and melodic material when performing
   b) explore, choose, combine and organise musical ideas within musical structures

Responding and reviewing – appraising skills
3. Pupils should be taught how to:
   a) analyse and compare sounds
   b) explore and explain their own ideas and feelings about music using movement, dance and expressive language and musical vocabulary
   c) improve their own and others' work in relation to its intended effort

Listening, and applying knowledge and understanding
4. Pupils should be taught:
   a) to listen with attention to detail and to internalise and recall sounds with increasing aural memory
   b) how the combined musical elements of pitch, duration, dynamics, tempo, timbre, texture and silence can be organised within musical structures (for example, ostinato) and used to communicate different moods and effects
   c) how music is produced in different ways (for example, through the use of different resources, including ICT) and described through relevant established and invented notations
   d) how time and place can influence the way music is created, performed and heard (for example, the effect of occasion and venue)

Breadth of study

5. During the key stage pupils should be taught the **knowledge, skills and understanding** through:
   a) a range of musical activities that integrate performing, composing and appraising
   b) responding to a range of musical and non-musical starting points
   c) working on their own, in groups of different sizes and as a class
   d) using ICT to capture, change and combine sounds
   e) a range of live and recorded music from different times and cultures (for example, from the British Isles, from classical, folk and popular genres, by well-known composers and performers)

Crown Copyright material is reproduced with the permission of the Controller of HMSO and the Queen's Printer for Scotland. Qualifications and Curriculum Authority copyright material is reproduced under the terms of HMSO Guidance Note 8.

Appendices

Glossary of Musical Terms

Accent	a note played or sung more forcefully
Accelerando	getting gradually faster
Bar	grouping of notes into small units for ease of reading
Bar line	a vertical line showing the end of a bar on the stave
Beat	the regular pulse in music
Bebop	a form of jazz characterized by fast tempos and improvisation
Big Band	an ensemble associated with playing jazz, particularly swing (see swing)
Blues	music based on the use of blue notes , usually with a twelve-bar structure
Boogie Woogie	a type of fast blues (see blues) played on solo piano with a walking bass
Brass	name of a section of the orchestra
Canon	playing/singing in a round
Conductor	the musical director of a group of singers or players
Crescendo	getting gradually louder
Diminuendo	getting gradually quieter
Dotted minim	a note lasting for three crotchets
Duration	the length of notes or rests
Dynamic(s)	loud and quiet in music
Ensemble	a small group of instruments playing together
Forte	loud
Fortissimo	very loud
Graphic score	music written using patterns and symbols
Imitation	a musical idea reappearing later in a piece in a slightly different guise.
Internalising	hearing the music inside your head
Interval	the distance between two pitched notes, e.g. *step, skip*
Intonation	singing/playing in tune
Jazz	a type of music of African American origin
Lento	very slow
Melody	the tune
Metre	the number of beats in the bar
Mezzo Forte	moderately loud
Mezzo Piano	moderately quiet
Moderato	at a medium speed
Octave	eight notes
Orchestra	large group of instruments playing together
Ostinato	repeated pattern of notes as an accompaniment
Percussion	name of a section of the orchestra
Phrase	musical sentence
Piano	quiet
Pianissimo	very quiet
Pitch	whether the sound is high or low
Pizzicato	plucked
Presto	very fast
Pulse	another word for beat
Ragtime	music mainly for piano with a distinctive pattern in the bass and a syncopated melody (see syncopation)
Rallentando	getting gradually slower

Rest	a period of silence in music
Rhythm	the pattern of short and long sounds
Rumba	a Cuban dance with a distinctive rhythmic pattern
Semibreve	a note lasting for four crotchets
Semiquavers	half quavers
Sol-fa	the name of a system to help you learn to sing in tune
Solo	one voice or instrument alone
Stave	the five lines on which music notes are written
Strings	name of a section of the orchestra
Staccato	very short (detached) sounds
Structure	the way a piece of music is put together
Swing	a type of jazz with a strong rhythm section including double bass and drums, medium to fast tempo and distinctive swing-time rhythm
Syncopation	a strong sound on a weak beat
Texture	layers of sound in music
Tied notes	notes joined together by a tie to make a continuous sound
Timbre	the quality of sound of different instruments
Time signature	a symbol showing the number of beats in a bar
Treble clef	the symbol at the beginning of a stave on which the middle range and higher notes are written
Woodwind	name of a section of the orchestra

Assessment Grids

- The next two pages provide you with photocopiable sheets for assessment.
- Use the first one at the end of every lesson. The names of the children in your class should be written down the left hand side. The date should be written at the top of each column. Simply write a quick comment against a child's name if there is something that particularly struck you during the lesson, e.g. 'Jonno didn't want to work with Fred' or 'Jamie contributed loads to prep of improv' or 'Anna loved the song' etc
- These notes, combined with your own build-up of observation about the children in all the many and varied activities they do over the period of a half term, will then help you to fill in the second sheet at the end of each half term for each individual child. It covers very basic and obvious musical skills and you will now be able and equipped to make a judgement on each heading provided you have devised lessons along the lines of the set lessons given for each year group.
- Don't worry about not relating to the specific National Curriculum levels directly. With this method you will be covering all the National Curriculum content and more!

Name	Date			
Name	Date			

Appendices

Name		Year	Form

Date			
Sense of pitch			
Sense of rhythm			
Singing/playing/ moving expressively			
Listening			
Working in a group			
Concentration			
Co-ordination			
Performance skills			
Imagination (e.g. when preparing an improvisation)			
Appraising skills/ability to be self-critical			

CD Track Listing

and the first reference in the book to each track

 CD 1

1	Listen to the beat (year 3, lesson 1)
2	Four different beats played at once (year 3, lesson 1)
3	*Chop Chop!* (vocal) (year 3, lesson 1)
4	*Chop Chop!* (accompaniment) (year 3, lesson 2)
5	Four sets of eight *sol-fa* sequences (year 3, lesson 3)
6	The pitch game – ten examples (year 3, lesson 4)
7	Dustman's Drudge (year 4, lesson 1)
8	*Magic Carpet* (vocal) (year 4, lesson 1)
9	*Magic Carpet* (accompaniment) (year 4, lesson 2)
10	Sound of the flute (year 4, lesson 3)
11	Sound of the oboe (year 4, lesson 3)
12	Sound of the clarinet (year 4, lesson 3)
13	Sound of the bassoon (year 4, lesson 3)
14	Sound of the trumpet (year 4, lesson 3)
15	Sound of the trombone (year 4, lesson 3)
16	Sound of the horn (year 4, lesson 3)
17	Sound of the violin (year 4, lesson 3)
18	Sound of the cello (year 4, lesson 3)
19	Sound of the double bass (year 4, lesson 3)
20	Sound of the bass drum (year 4, lesson 3)
21	Sound of the kettle drum (year 4, lesson 3)
22	Sound of the snare drum (year 4, lesson 3)
23	Rhythms with semiquavers (year 5, lesson 1)
24	*Now is Now* (vocal) (year 5, lesson 2)
25	*Now is Now* (accompaniment) (year 5, lesson 4)
26	Extract of Twelve-bar blues music (year 6, lesson 1)
27	Extract of Boogie Woogie (year 6, lesson 1)
28	*Getting' in the Groove* A jazz piece (year 6, lesson 1)
29	Drum kit (year 6, lesson 1)
30	Extract of Ragtime (year 6, lesson 2)
31	Extract of Dixieland Trad. (year 6, lesson 2)
32	Extract of Swing (year 6, lesson 2)
33	Extract of Bebop (year 6, lesson 2)
34	Extract of Big Band (year 6, lesson 2)
35	*Sing an' Jump Up for Joy* (vocal) (year 6, lesson 2)
36	*Sing an' Jump Up for Joy* (accompaniment) (year 6, lesson 4)
37	Making beats from a poem (Mix and Match: Rhythmic Work)
38	Speaking in canon (Mix and Match: Rhythmic Work)
39	*Right Royal Rap* (Mix and Match: Rhythmic Work)
40	*Right Royal Rap* (backing track)
41	*Pig Rap* (Mix and Match: Rhythmic Work)
42	*Pig Rap* (backing track)
43	Two songs at once (vocal) (Mix and Match: Pitch Work)

 CD 2

1	*Magic Spells* (vocal) (Mix and Match: Songs)
2	*Magic Spells* (accompaniment)
3	*Thread of my Dreams* (vocal) (Mix and Match: Songs)
4	*Thread of my Dreams* (accompaniment)
5	*Spin the Straw* (vocal) (Mix and Match: Songs)
6	*Spin the Straw* (accompaniment)
7	*Seasons Turn to Seasons* (vocal) (Mix and Match: Songs)
8	*Seasons Turn to Seasons* (accompaniment)
9	*The Greatest Gran of All* (vocal) (Mix and Match: Songs)
10	*The Greatest Gran of All* (accompaniment)
11	*Fire!* (vocal) (Mix and Match: Songs)
12	*Fire!* (accompaniment)
13	*The Disco Beat* (vocal) (Mix and Match: Songs)
14	*The Disco Beat* (accompaniment)
15	*Rock 'n' Roll Boogie* (vocal) (Mix and Match: Songs)
16	*Rock 'n' Roll Boogie* (accompaniment)

Introducing Classical Music Through Stories

9702A
Wasp Alert in Minibug Bonanzaland

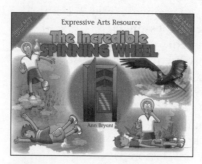

9703A
Incredible Spinning Wheel

9704A
William the crackshot kid

9933A
The Crazy Alien Ball

9934A
Billy Briggs, Big on Skates

9935A
Jupiter Cove

This series of six fully illustrated storybooks by Ann Bryant captures children's imaginations and introduces them to musical works through exciting adventure stories. Teachers can either read the story whilst playing the CD to help evoke the soundscape of the music; alternatively once pupils are familiar with the story they can simply listen and look at the pictures. The books are ideal for use as part of an integrated scheme of work for art, music and literacy and are an approachable resource for non-music-specialists.

- Aimed at primary children of all ages from Nursery upwards
- Great for use at home or school
- Perfect for both specialist and non-specialist teachers
- Stimulating resource for music, art and literacy
- Full of colourful illustrations
- CD of classical music included

"This is an inspiring resource for the literacy hour. Often those who work with primary age children sense an already reluctant attitude towards studying classical music, in particular the negative opinion that classical music is boring. This resource attempts successfully to dispel this myth. The clever fusion of inspiring music with a story and illustrations should prove to be an instant attraction."
Music Teacher Magazine

"Vaughan Williams' music, lavish illustration and a cleverly interwoven story all combine to make Wasp Alert in Minibug Bonanzaland a stimulating resource for infants and lower juniors."
Sheet Music Magazine